Making your Case: a Practical Guide to Essay Writing

Edited by Rebecca Stott, Anna Snaith and Rick Rylance

Series Editor: Rebecca Stott

Longman

An imprint of Pearson Education

Harlow, England · London · New York · Reading, Massachusetts · San Francisco · Toronto · Don Mills, Ontario · Sydney
Tokyo · Singapore · Hong Kong · Seoul · Taipei · Cape Town · Madrid · Mexico City · Amsterdam · Munich · Paris · Milan

Pearson Education Limited
Edinburgh Gate
Harlow
Essex CM20 2JE
England

and Associated Companies throughout the world

Visit us on the World Wide Web at:
http://www.pearsoneduc.com

_____

First published 2001

ISBN 0 582 38244 0

British Library Cataloguing-in-Publication Data
A catalogue record for this book is available from the British Library

Library of Congress Cataloging-in-Publication Data
Making your case : a practical guide to essay writing / edited by Rebecca Stott, Anna
Snaith and Rick Rylance.
     p. cm. — (Speak-write series)
     Includes index.
     ISBN 0-582-38244-0 (pbk.)
     1. English language—Rhetoric. 2. Essay—Authorship. 3. Report writing.
I. Stott, Rebecca. II. Snaith, Anna. III. Rylance, Rick. IV. Series.

PE1471.M24 2000
808.4—dc21
00-041204

10 9 8 7 6 5 4 3 2 1
04 03 02 01

Typeset by 35 in 10.5/12.5pt Janson Text
Printed and bound in Malaysia, LSP

CONTENTS

Making your Case: a Practical Guide to Essay Writing

SPEAK
WRITE
SERIES

Series Editor: DR REBECCA STOTT

Other titles in the series:

Grammar and Writing
Rebecca Stott and Peter Chapman (Eds)

Writing with Style
Rebecca Stott and Simon Avery (Eds)

Speaking your Mind: Oral Presentation and Seminar Skills
Rebecca Stott, Tory Young and Cordelia Bryan (Eds)

AUTHOR'S ACKNOWLEDGEMENTS

This book and the other three books in the Speak–Write Series, *Grammar and Writing*, *Writing with Style*, and *Speaking Your Mind: Oral Presentation and Seminar Skills*, have been three years in the making. They are the result of three years of research, teaching design and piloting undertaken by the Speak–Write Project, established by the English Department of Anglia Polytechnic University in Cambridge and funded by the Higher Education Funding Council for England through its Fund for the Development of Teaching and Learning. The Speak–Write Project was set up to respond to claims from members of English departments across the country that first-year undergraduates needed more intensive advanced writing and speaking courses at foundation level in order to perform more effectively in higher education.

Although the Speak–Write Project looked closely at freshman rhetoric and composition classes which have run successfully in the United States for decades, the Speak–Write designers and researchers concluded that there was a need in British higher education for innovative communication skills courses which were embedded in specific subject areas and not generic skills courses alone. These four books have been piloted, designed and adapted by and for lecturers and students working in English Literature departments and much of the material presented for analysis or rewriting or adaptation is of a literary kind. This said, the books have a much wider application and can be adapted for use by a range of cognate disciplines in the Humanities.

The Speak–Write books have drawn on the imagination, time and work of many people. The editors and authors of individual books and chapters are acknowledged beneath the chapter and book titles. Many more people and institutions have contributed who remain invisible and I would like to thank as many of them individually here as possible: Tory Young, Editorial

Assistant, who saw the books through their final metamorphosis, tirelessly and with great good humour and editorial skill; Ruth Maitland, the Speak–Write Project's Administrator, who held everything together; Rob Pope (Oxford Brookes University), Stephen Minta (York University), Val Purton (City College, Norwich), Morag Styles (Homerton College, Cambridge) and Katy Wales (Leeds University), external readers who assessed and advised on early drafts of the books; Paul Boyd, Richard James, Regine Hasseler, Shelby Bohland and Lucy Wood, the student editorial advisory group; Elizabeth Mann, Commissioning Editor at Longman, for her encouragement and enthusiasm for the Project in its early stages; staff and students of the English Department at Anglia Polytechnic University who have refined and shaped the books through giving continual feedback on aspects of teaching and learning; and my first-year students of 1999 in particular for applying their minds to difficult editorial decisions.

Finally, Rick Rylance would like to thank Chris Kirkham particularly for a contribution to Chapter 6.

Rebecca Stott, *Series Editor*

PUBLISHER'S ACKNOWLEDGEMENTS

We are grateful to the following for permission to reproduce copyright material:

Authors' agents Curtis Brown for the article 'Composition, Distribution, Arrangement: Form and Structure in Jane Austen's Novels' from *AFTER BAKHTIN: ESSAYS ON FICTION AND CRITICISM* by David Lodge, published by Routledge © David Lodge 1990; Guardian Newspapers Ltd for the article 'Digested Read: Men are from Mars' in the Editor Section in *THE GUARDIAN*; Jacob Morrish for the interview 'What makes a good essay?' and Stanford University Press for an extract from *THE COMPLETE ESSAYS OF MONTAIGNE* translated by Donald M. Frame © 1958 by the Board of Trustees for the Leland Stanford Junior University.

INTRODUCTION

Rebecca Stott

The bodily eye, the organ for apprehending material objects, is provided by nature; the eye of the mind, of which the object is truth, is the work of discipline and habit.

(John Henry Newman, *The Idea of a University*, 1852)

This book began life as materials prepared for first-year English literature students studying on a module called Varieties of Writing, an intensive writing course pioneered in the English Department of Anglia Polytechnic University (APU), Cambridge. At that point academic essay writing was only one of the 'varieties of writing' being studied by students enrolled on the module. As the course progressed, the course designers, tutors and students came to realise that going behind the scenes to look closely at the numerous techniques involved in the processes of academic writing in particular was a complicated task. We consulted with students at APU and elsewhere about what they wanted from such a first-year course on academic writing. Most said that they wanted the processes of writing to be demystified: although the academic essay was central to individual achievement in higher education, it seemed to be an activity that went on outside rather than inside seminar and tutorial rooms. Students wanted an opportunity to investigate and learn about the process of writing itself as an integral part of their education. This book on academic writing is rooted in the study of literature because it was developed by and with English students, but its usefulness is not confined to English. The techniques and strategies we explore apply to all courses which require a degree of argumentation and analysis. The business of arguing and persuading, of making a case and supporting it with detailed and relevant evidence, is the daily business of students studying a range of different subjects in higher education.

So this book is about putting writing at the centre of higher education and demystifying the business of writing an academic essay for assessment. There are many students entering higher education who feel that the ability to write is something that either has or has not been bequeathed them, like gifts from the fairies. We have begun with the principle that essay writing, like all genres of writing, has a function and a history and that it is a craft like any other, a craft that can be learned with practice and reflection. This book is designed to help you think of yourself as a writer and to reflect on your craft as you develop. Working through the book systematically should help you to tackle your assignments more confidently and with a greater sense of the range of approaches and techniques available to you.

Occasionally, students approach tutors to ask to be taught how to get a first-class mark for their essays. This book does not claim to give you a formula for doing so, because there is no such formula to give. There are as many ways of getting a first-class mark as there are ways of failing. But what we can give you is an opportunity to reflect on the good practice of students and academics who do already write effectively, and thereby to enhance your skills.

Over the last decade many changes have taken place in higher education. Many departments have broadened the ways in which they test their students' abilities as writers and thinkers so that assessment methods often now include not just exams and essays but oral presentations, portfolios, dissertations and reviews. Although each of these tasks makes different demands upon the writer, to some extent most require complex skills in preparing, organising and presenting material. Being a successful thinker and writer is partly about acquiring relevant information but is more importantly about being able to *transform* that knowledge into a new kind of understanding which you can express clearly. This process of transformation is most often achieved by the application of pen to paper or fingers to keyboard. In the words of John Henry Newman, here defending higher education in the middle of the nineteenth century:

> it is not mere application, however exemplary, which introduces the mind to truth, nor the reading many books, nor the getting up many subjects, nor the witnessing many experiments, nor the attending many lectures. All this is short of enough; a man may have done it all, yet be lingering in the vestibule of knowledge . . .
>
> (Newman 1996: 37)

Newman claims that understanding comes through discipline and habit, through 'the comparison, the combination, the mutual correction, the continual adaptation, of many partial notions'. We have also placed a great deal of emphasis in this book on drafting and redrafting, on adaptation and correction as essential processes in the transformation and communication of ideas.

Moving beyond knowledge to understanding, discriminating between one idea and another, building up ideas to make a case, these are the skills central to academic essay writing and also to the ancient arts of rhetoric. For these reasons, we have placed argument and the underpinning of argument by evidence at the heart of this book. We begin in Chapters 1 and 2 by introducing you to the history and variety of the essay as a genre, as well as to the range of styles and voices employed by contemporary critics and students. In Chapters 3 and 4 we take you through the processes of academic writing in detail, stage by stage, from brainstorming to proofreading. In Chapters 5 and 6 we concentrate on summary and editing skills, giving you a chance to practice these skills by rewriting extracts. Chapter 7 provides a guide to the three different systems of referencing currently used in academic writing.

How to use this book

We have structured the book carefully and progressively and we will often be referring back to parts we have already covered and forward to items not yet dealt with. Broadly speaking, then, we are advising you not just to *read*, but to *work through* the sequences of steps and examples from Chapters 1 to 7. Some of the activities will be more demanding (in terms of time and level of difficulty) than others. Most chapters have about ten to twelve activities to complete, each of which will enhance your understanding of the material in the chapter in different ways, and most activities can be adapted for use by either individuals or groups. However, a few are group-only activities because they are based on discussion. We have provided enough activities in each chapter for readers to choose those which best suit their particular needs, interests and circumstances.

Reference

Newman, John Henry (1996) *The Idea of a University* [1852], ed. Frank M. Turner, Martha McMackin Garland, Sara Castro Klaren, George P. Landow and George M. Marsden. Yale: Yale University Press.

On essays

Anna Snaith

Questions of definition

The aim of this book is to help you develop and improve your academic essay writing skills. As you work through the book you will concentrate on the importance of argument in essays, as well as the various components of the essay: beginnings and endings, paragraph structure, use of secondary sources and referencing. Before focusing specifically on the academic essay, however, it will be helpful to consider the genre of the essay itself. Looking at the variety of essays – satiric, journalistic, verse, moralistic, political – will help to differentiate the academic essay from these other types. It is important to keep in mind that the essay is a varied form and that the kinds of essays you write during the course of your study represent one type among many.

What is an essay? You most likely read essays in the newspaper, in journals or in books of criticism. It is very hard to offer a useful definition of the essay, however. Of all genres, it is perhaps the most variable, flexible and heterogeneous. Essays relate to and incorporate many other forms of writing, such as autobiography, satire and fiction. Since the essayist often speaks in his or her own voice, essays raise questions about how the self, or individual identity, is portrayed through writing. Essays can also blur the boundary between fiction and non-fiction. Can essays be literary and non-fictional?

First, let's think about the roots (etymology) of the word 'essay': maybe that will help us define the genre. The word's French root is 'essayer', meaning to try, to attempt or to experiment. Its Latin root, 'exagium', means 'weighing' an object or an idea, seeing it from different angles. The essay, therefore, is a forum for trying out ideas, for putting forward a case or developing an argument. An essay is an attempt to answer a question, or questions, but importantly it is an *attempt*, not the final word. If you are writing an essay on *Hamlet*, for example, you are putting forward your opinions, or your reading, of the play. You need to have an argument and you need to back up that argument with evidence, but you don't expect every reader to agree with it. Since the essayist writes in his/her own voice, the essay is necessarily that – one person's opinion, however well-argued or persuasive that opinion may be.

Varying definitions have been offered for the essay, but as we will see, the purpose, form and tone of essays have changed over history, so that no definition is all-encompassing. The essay has been called a 'short, non-fiction prose form' (Obaldia 1995: 11). This definition allows for complete diversity of subject and content: it makes no stipulations regarding the essayist's subject matter, or how s/he will write. On the other hand, there have been book-length essays, and essays in verse. Michael Holroyd, the biographer, has offered the definition: 'a non-fiction short story'. Although this seems contradictory (how can a short story be non-fiction?), it foregrounds this tension in the essay genre between creative and non-fictional writing. What these definitions highlight is the difficulty in finding an accurate, inclusive definition, simply because the essay is such a heterogeneous form. As we will see, the essay can be a hundred words long, or a hundred pages long; it can be personal and informal, or aloof and didactic in tone; it can be written in verse or prose; it can take the form of a letter, a dialogue, a character sketch, a memoir, travel literature, a treatise or an anecdote.

The essay in history

Many Classical writers, even though they were writing before the term 'essay' had been coined, wrote what later came to be called essays. Theophrastus' *Characters* (third century BC), Seneca's *Epistle to Lucilius* (second century AD) and Marcus Aurelius' *The Meditations* (second century AD) are just a few examples of texts which could be considered essays and which would have influenced Michel de Montaigne's 'invention' of the genre.

The 'first' essayist

The person who first used the term 'essay' was a French writer called Michel de Montaigne (1533–92). He was not the first person to write what we now call essays, but he was the person who attached the name to the form, publishing a book entitled *Essais* (*Essays*) in 1580. What was new about his essays was their focus on himself: the opinions and experiences of one man. His essays, then, directly express Renaissance concerns: the emphasis on the individual and his place in the outside world. His general argument throughout the essays is that man must accept both his body and soul, as well as his limitations. Once his limitations are confronted, then through order, calm and kindness he can achieve his full potential as a human being.

Montaigne wrote essays on a wide range of subjects, such as idleness, friendship and sleep. The purpose always seems to be to 'assay' his own value, his opinions, his behaviour, his habits. The more essays Montaigne wrote, the longer and more personal they became. He began to allow himself more freedom within the form to digress. Montaigne's essays are extremely accessible and informal. He wanted to write in everyday language, so as not to alienate readers. Although he is the focus of his essays, they are not egocentric. He scrutinises himself out of curiosity, rather than vanity or arrogance. The essays are all about dialogue and communication with the reader. He invites the reader to join in the discussion. Many commentators on Montaigne's essays have noted how easily the reader identifies with the writer.

In his preface 'To The Reader', Montaigne clearly sets out his intention in publishing his essays. He writes: 'I am myself the matter of my book', but that, importantly, 'I want to be seen here in my simple, natural, ordinary fashion, without straining or artifice . . . My defects will here be read to the life' (Montaigne 1965: 2). The essays are not written for self-glorification, but so that his friends and relatives will be able to remember him when he dies. His aim is to present his ideas, behaviour, likes and dislikes in an honest, open manner. The essays, then, function like a self-portrait.

ACTIVITY 1:

In groups, analyse the following opening paragraph from Montaigne's essay 'Of the Power of the Imagination'. Is there a key argument or claim in the paragraph? How would you summarise it in one sentence? How is comparison used to strengthen the claims of the paragraph? How is the imagination characterised? How is the personal interwoven with the general? What kind of language does Montaigne use?

> *A strong imagination creates the event,* say the scholars. I am one of those who are very much influenced by the imagination. Everyone feels its impact, but some are overthrown by it. Its impression on me is piercing. And my art is to escape it, not to resist it. I would live solely in the presence of gay, healthy people. The sight of other people's anguish causes very real anguish to me, and my feelings have often usurped the feelings of others. A continual cougher irritates my lungs and throat. I visit less willingly the sick toward whom duty directs me than those toward whom I am less attentive and concerned. I catch the disease that I study, and lodge it in me. I do not find it strange that imagination brings fevers and death to those who give it a free hand and encourage it.

(Montaigne 1965: 68)

ACTIVITY 2:

Below is the whole of Montaigne's essay 'Of Idleness'. Read it through carefully. Here is a paraphrase of the main claim of the opening paragraph: 'Just as land must be cultivated to produce crops and women must be fertilised to produce children, the mind can only be productive if it thinks about a particular subject in an ordered fashion'. Reduce the second paragraph of Montaigne's essay ('Lately...itself.') to a sentence which summarises the main claim of the paragraph. Compare your paraphrase to the original. What has been lost or gained in this paraphrase? What is it about Montaigne's prose style that makes his essays so enjoyable to read?

Just as we see that fallow land, if rich and fertile, teems with a hundred thousand kinds of wild and useless weeds, and that to set it to work we must subject it and sow it with certain seeds for our service; and as we see that women, all alone, produce mere shapeless masses and lumps of flesh, but that to create a good and natural offspring they must be made fertile with a different kind of seed; so it is with minds. Unless you keep them busy with some definite subject that will bridle and control them, they throw themselves in disorder hither and yon in the vague field of imagination.

> Thus, in a brazen urn, the water's light
> Trembling reflects the sun's and moon's bright rays,
> And, darting here and there in aimless flight,
> Rises aloft, and on the ceiling plays. (Virgil)

And there is no mad or idle fancy that they do not bring forth in this agitation:

> Like a sick man's dreams,
> They form vain visions. (Horace)

The soul that has no fixed goal loses itself; for as they say, to be everywhere is to be nowhere:

> He who dwells everywhere, Maximus, nowhere dwells. (Martial)

Lately when I retired to my home, determined so far as possible to bother about nothing except spending the little life I have left in rest and seclusion, it seemed to me I could do my mind no greater favour than to let it entertain itself in full idleness and stay and settle in itself, which I hoped it might do more easily now, having become weightier and riper with time. But I find –

> Ever idle hours breed wandering thoughts (Lucan)

– that, on the contrary, like a runaway horse, it gives itself a hundred times more trouble than it took for others, and gives birth to so many chimeras and fantastic monsters, one after another, without order or purpose, that in order to contemplate their ineptitude and strangeness at my pleasure, I have begun to put them in writing, hoping in time to make my mind ashamed of itself.

(Montaigne 1965: 20–1)

ACTIVITY 3:

Read the essay 'On Idleness' through again and consider the follow questions. Write up your answers as a short report.

- What is the thesis, claim or main argument of the essay in full? How does it link with the opening of the essay on imagination?
- What evidence does Montaigne use to support his claims? Where does he gather his evidence from?
- Summarise the claims that you think Montaigne is making with each of the quotations. Do you think that Montaigne uses quotations effectively?
- Who are the people whom Montaigne quotes? (If you do not recognise the names, use an encyclopaedia to find out who they are.) What do they have in common? Why do you think Montaigne draws on the writings of these people in particular?
- How does Montaigne use analogy? How does he portray women within this context?
- How does he represent his own idleness? How does the first-person voice, the 'I', work within the essay?
- Why is Montaigne's essay successful? Consider his use of tone, style, rhythm and diction, as well as his powers of persuasion and argument.

After Montaigne

In the century after Montaigne published his essays, many British writers were heavily influenced by Montaigne's ideas. Francis Bacon (1561–1626) was a British philosopher and statesman, who followed Montaigne's lead, publishing *The Essays, or Counsels, Civil and Moral* in 1597. This first book contained ten essays, the second published in 1612 contained thirty-eight and then a book of fifty-eight came out in 1625. In contrast to Montaigne, Bacon's essays are more formal and didactic, and the tone is distant and objective rather than intimate. They are short, often only several hundred words in length. He described his essays as 'grains of salt which will rather give an appetite than offend with satiety' (Cuddon 1977: 239). They are tasters, the beginning of a discussion rather than a comprehensive account. The essays offer advice on how one should live life most profitably or successfully. The dedication to his 1625 collection read: 'My essays, which of all my other works have been most current; for that as it seems they come home to men's business, and bosoms' (Bacon 1985: 57). Their popularity lies in the fact that they deal with everyday affairs and emotions.

Let's look at the beginning of Bacon's essay 'Of Revenge', which appeared in the 1625 collection:

> Revenge is a kind of wild justice; which the more man's nature runs to, the more ought law to weed it out. For as for the first wrong, it doth but offend the law; but the revenge of that wrong putteth the law out of office. Certainly, in taking revenge, a man is but even with his enemy; but in passing it over, he is superior; for it is a prince's part to pardon . . .

> (Gross 1991: 3)

The essay is only a page long, and sets about analysing the nature of revenge, its different forms, and situations in which it occurs. Like Montaigne, Bacon uses quotation and examples to illustrate his points. The thesis or argument of the essay, however, is that revenge is wrong, and that the morally advanced person will pass over the wrongs done to him/her and look to the future rather than the past. The essay ends with the claim: 'vindictive persons live the life of witches; who, as they are mischievous, so end they unfortunate'. The essay is clearly didactic, working on a Christian rhetoric of good and evil, hence the biblical quotations and allusions in the body of the essay. From these extracts, we can see how formal and abstracted Bacon's style is; the ideas are his opinions, but he does not use personal examples like Montaigne. The voice is authoritative, rather than intimate.

In England in the seventeenth and eighteenth centuries, the essay came into its own. The essay form itself diversified. John Locke (1632–1704), for example, published his book-length *Essay Concerning Human Understanding* in 1690, which was a philosophical treatise on the origin and nature of human knowledge and the relationship between faith and reason. In 1668, John Dryden, while living in Wiltshire to escape the plague in London, wrote his *Essay of Dramatic Poesy*, which took the form of a symposium, or a discussion between four friends on such subjects as rhyme, Shakespeare and English versus French drama. Again, we are seeing what a diverse genre the essay is; it can be dramatic, narrative, nostalgic, philosophical, moralistic.

Periodical essays

In general, in the late seventeenth and eighteenth centuries the essay became a more popular form, in that more essayists wrote to entertain rather than to teach or advise. Literacy rose, as people had more leisure time in which to read. Periodicals flourished in which essayists could publish their work. The best-known writers of such essays were Joseph Addison (1672–1719) and Richard Steele (1672–1729), who published in periodicals called the *Tatler* (1709–11) and the *Spectator* (1711–13). The subjects of their essays were diverse, including women's hats, Westminster Abbey and their own childhood. These essays are for amusement and relaxation, and are characterised by range of interest and acute observation, rather than deep, moral 'truth'. Their subject matter was more domestic and social than rigorously political or literary. They made the essay a more popular form. Addison once said: 'I shall be ambitious to have it said of me, that I have brought philosophy out of closets and libraries, schools and colleges, to dwell in clubs and assemblies, at tea-tables and coffee-houses'. The essay was the means by which he achieved this goal.

Here is the opening of Addison's essay 'Sir Roger in Westminster Abbey' (1712):

> My friend Sir Roger de Coverley told me the other night, that he had been reading my paper upon Westminster Abbey, in which, says he, there are a great many ingenious fancies. He told me at the same time, that he observed I had promised another paper upon the tombs, and that he should be glad to go and see them with me . . . Accordingly I called upon him the next morning, that we might go together to the Abbey.
>
> (Gross 1991: 46–7)

Several interesting things are going on here. First, the essay has become self-reflexive. Addison refers to one of his previous essays, 'Thoughts in Westminster Abbey' (1711), and the reaction which it received. A dialogue is set up between Addison's essays. Secondly, we see here how the essay is a hybrid genre. This essay could very well be described as a *short story*: it has characters and a narrative, since it tells the story of Addison and de Coverley's trip round Westminster Abbey. Its focus is de Coverley's reaction to the tombs in the Abbey. The essay, therefore, is also a *character sketch* of de Coverley. We learn about de Coverley's 'honest passion for the glory of his country', his 'benevolence' and 'good humour'. Compared to the Bacon excerpt, Addison's is highly personal and anecdotal; it focuses upon one incident in the friendship of the two men.

In addition to the *Tatler* and the *Spectator*, Daniel Defoe's (1661–1731) *Review*, published between 1704 and 1713, was full of essays, including his own. Defoe would read his essays aloud on street corners both to air his political opinions and to make money. Samuel Johnson's (1709–84) periodical the *Rambler* was another home for the essay. It was published twice a week between 1750 and 1752. Johnson's essays were much more moralistic than Addison and Steele's.

Verse essays

It is worth looking in more detail at Alexander Pope (1688–1744) as a poet who wrote essays in verse. His 'An Essay on Criticism' (1711), written when he was only twenty-three, is a 700-line verse essay on ideas of taste, and how critics should be guided. It is written entirely in heroic couplets. His 'Essay on Man' (1733–34) is a verse essay in four epistles on the individual's relation to the universe and society, upholding the rightness of the world as ordered by God. Despite Pope's persecution because of his Catholicism (he was forced to live outside London), he maintained the importance of the poet in public life. He saw it as his duty to write about, and satirise, what he saw as the loss of order, reason and cultural values. Style is content for Pope. His verse itself is ordered and balanced, pithy and memorable. Many well-known aphorisms have their origins in his work, such as:

> A little learning is a dangerous thing;
> Drink deep, or taste not the Pierian spring:
> There shallow draughts intoxicate the brain,
> And drinking largely sobers us again.

('An Essay on Criticism', ll. 215–18; Pope 1972: 73–4)

The last lines of his 'Essay on Man' provide an interesting perspective on the autobiographical element of essay writing:

> Thou wert my guide, philosopher, and friend?
> That, urged by thee, I turn'd the tuneful art
> From sounds to things, from fancy to the heart;
> For Wit's false mirror held up Nature's light;
> Show'd erring Pride, – Whatever is, is right!
> That reason, passion, answer one great aim;
> That true self-love and social are the same;
> That virtue only makes our bliss below;
> And all our knowledge is, – Ourselves to know.

(Pope 1972: 232)

One of the purposes of art, and this essay, for Pope, is self-exploration, both as an individual and in his public role. Writing allows him to look inward, and to speak outwardly. It gives him a public voice. He is, however, not looking at himself as a unique individual (the essay is not personal in that sense), but at mankind in general. In examining himself, he examines the whole of society, for the claim of the last lines of his 'Essay on Man' is that 'self-love and social are the same'. Poetry used within the essay form allows him to use lyrical language to serve a rhetorical purpose, the revelation of a virtuous way of living and the order inherent in the world.

Pseudonyms

As Renaissance individualism began to decline, essayists often used pseudonyms or wrote anonymously in order to establish a rapport with their readers and because the personal identity of the writer was not considered important. Anonymity also meant, of course, that writers could write more critically. The Irish satirist Jonathan Swift signed himself 'A Drapier' in *The Drapier's Letters* (1724–25) and pretended to be an economist in *A Modest Proposal* (1729), both highly controversial and critical commentaries on the state of Ireland. The first three epistles of Pope's 'Essay on Man' were published anonymously. Charles Lamb contributed essays to *The London Magazine* between 1820 and 1823 under the pseudonym of 'the gentle Elia', the name of a fellow clerk, and nearly all of the great Victorians published in the leading periodicals of the day wrote anonymously.

Many women essayists in the nineteenth century used a pseudonym in order to assume a male identity which made it easier for them to proffer opinions on contemporary issues. Women writers were often criticised as being unfeminine if their writing was political in any way. From 1851 to 1854 Marian Evans (George Eliot) was assistant editor of the *Westminster Review*, a leading intellectual journal of the day, and from 1854 to 1857 she also wrote long essays for the journal and was a regular reviewer of contemporary literature. In these essays she wrote extensively about the aims and methods of nineteenth-century novelists, working out her artistic credo before she began to write fiction herself in 1856, taking the pseudonym George Eliot for the first time.

ACTIVITY 4:

Read the opening paragraph of George Eliot's essay 'Thomas Carlyle' (1855):

> It has been well said that the highest aim in education is analogous to the highest aim in Mathematics, namely, to obtain not *results* but *powers*, not particular solutions, but the means by which endless solutions may be wrought. He is the most effective educator who aims less at perfecting specific acquirements than at producing that mental condition which renders acquirements easy, and leads to their useful application; who does not seek to make his pupils moral by enjoining particular courses of action, but by bringing into activity the feelings and sympathies that must issue in noble action. On the same ground it may be said that the most effective writer is not he who announces a particular discovery, who convinces men of a particular conclusion, who demonstrates that this measure is right and that measure wrong; but he who rouses in others the activities that must issue in discovery, who awakes men from their indifference to the right and the wrong, who nerves their energies to seek for the truth and live up to it at whatever cost. The influence of such a writer is dynamic. He does not teach men how to use sword and

musket, but he inspires their souls with courage and sends a strong will into their muscles. He does not, perhaps, enrich your stock of data, but he clears away the film from your eyes that you may search for data to some purpose. He does not, perhaps, convince you, but he strikes you, undeceives you, animates you. You are not directly fed by his books, but you are braced as by a walk up to an alpine summit, and yet subdued to calm and reverence as by the sublime things to be seen from that summit.

Such a writer is Thomas Carlyle...

(Gross 1991: 239)

Analyse this opening paragraph and write up your answers to the following questions in the form of a short report:

- What is Eliot's main claim in this paragraph?
- Summarise the claim or claims of the paragraph in one clear sentence. Do Eliot's ideas follow on from one another?
- How does she persuade the reader of her argument?
- Does she present any counter-arguments?
- What evidence does she use to support her claims?
- How does the paragraph work as a lead in to the discussion of Carlyle's writing?

The 'perfect' essay

Essays are studied on contemporary English literature courses but they are often considered non-literary or on the margins of literature, mainly useful for contextual purposes, and are seen as taking second place to genres such as the novel, play or poem. From the nineteenth century essays have been used to teach people to write well, as examples of perfected prose. This use of the essay is all very well, but it led to notions of the 'perfect' essay. This detracts from what we have seen to be the strength of the essay genre: its variety and freedom. In *Our Mutual Friend*, Dickens (1812–70) satirises this notion of the perfectibility of the essay in the following description of the schoolteacher Miss Peecher:

Small, shining, neat, methodical and buxom was Miss Peecher; cheery-cheeked and tuneful of voice. A little pincushion, a little housewife, a little book, a little workbox, a little set of tables and weights and measures and a little woman all in one. She could write a little Essay on any subject, exactly a slate long, beginning at the left hand top of one side and ending at the right hand bottom of the other, and the Essay should be strictly according to rule. If Mr. Bradley Headstone had addressed a written proposal of marriage to her, she would probably have replied in a complete little Essay on the theme, exactly a slate long, but would certainly have replied yes.

(Dickens 1981: 219)

Dickens satirises Miss Peecher's pedagogy here in that we assume she gets her students to write equally rigid and constrained essays. To write essays according to such rules seems to go against the versatility of the form. The content of Miss Peecher's essays is restricted by the length of the slate. The expression and testing of ideas and arguments has become subordinated to space restrictions, and this appears to be the only way in which Miss Peecher can express herself. Dickens is also making a point about register and context. An essay is not an appropriate form through which to reply to a proposal of marriage.

Self-reflexivity: essays on essays

Walter Pater (1839–94), an essayist, critic and novelist, who wrote largely on literature, philosophy and the fine arts, also wrote about the essay form itself. In his work *Plato and Platonism*, published in the 1890s, he argued that the essay was the perfect genre for the expression of ideas. Furthermore, he argued that the essay was the 'invention of the relative, or modern spirit' (Pater 1910: 174). Pater argued that all truth is relative, or contingent, and that the essay is a form which leaves room for inconclusivity. An essayist can express multiple viewpoints, or arguments; the essay embodies Pater's idea of 'lifelong, endless dialogue' (Pater 1910: 192). Like Montaigne's essays, such work invites a dialogue or dialectic with the reader. It does not present ideas as the final answer or the one-and-only, authoritative perspective. This is something to remember when writing your own essays: that as much as you want your essay to have an argument and to present that argument convincingly, you need to acknowledge and allow for counter-arguments and varying interpretations.

In the twentieth century, writers became even more self-conscious about the essay genre itself. The Hungarian, Marxist critic Georg Lukács wrote 'On the Nature and Form of the Essay' (1910), published in his book *Soul and Form*. Lukács (1885–1971) highlights the idea of the essay as a process rather than an end-result: 'The essay is a judgement, but the essential, the value-determining thing about it is not the verdict ... but the process of judging' (Lukács 1974: 18). The essay, as a form, takes the reader through that process. The essay is a journey of ideas between writer and reader. It allows the reader to trace the writer's thought-patterns, ideas and opinions. That process, then, needs to be clearly laid out and ideas need to follow from each other. As you hone your own essay writing skills, you need to imagine that you are the reader. Have you structured your ideas so that the reader can follow your thought-processes? Lukács also stresses the importance of the voice and personality of the writer in the essay writing process. He writes:

The essayist dismisses his own proud hopes which sometimes lead him to believe that he has come close to the ultimate: he has, after all, no more to offer than explanations of the poems of others, or at best of his own ideas.

(Lukács 1974: 9)

Lukács is writing here about essays of literary criticism, but his ideas are applicable to all kinds of essays. The essayist is only offering his or her own ideas, rather than authoritative truths about a given subject. The essayist must 'become conscious of his own self, must find himself and build something of his own out of himself'. Interestingly, Lukács's essay is written as a letter. By framing the essay this way, he foregrounds the flexibility of the essay's form.

Gender and the essay

Virginia Woolf (1882–1941) was a prolific essayist. As a woman, denied a formal education, she had to overcome patriarchal assumptions about women and writing. Many women writers in the nineteenth century had to publish under male pseudonyms just to get their work accepted and read. It was assumed that women, if they wrote at all, wrote light romances or popular fiction. The essay, then, with its propensity for serious literary, philosophical or political topics, was hardly seen as a suitable medium for a woman writer. Woolf wrote her first review in 1904 for the *Guardian*, an Anglo-Catholic paper. She quickly branched out and wrote for the *Times Literary Supplement*, as well as other periodicals. These reviews were published anonymously, which allowed Woolf to develop her public voice and air her opinions more forcefully.

She also quickly began to publish short, signed essays on various subjects, such as 'street music' and 'laughter', as well as essays on essay writing itself. In 'The Decay of Essay Writing', Woolf, like Pater, argues that despite the long history of essay writing, the huge number of essayists is a modern phenomenon. The essay is 'something of our own – typical, characteristic, a sign of the times' (Woolf 1986: 25). In 'The Modern Essay', she argues also that 'as the conditions change so the essayist, most sensitive of all plants to public opinion, adapts himself' (Woolf 1975: 274). This sense that so many prolific essayists have, that the essay is somehow a sign of their times, or that their age has re-invented it, is again evidence of the flexibility of the form: that it can be re-worked to suit different historical periods. Woolf acknowledges the heterogeneity of the essay: 'The form, too, admits variety. The essay can be short or long, serious or trifling, about God and Spinoza, or about turtles and Cheapside' (Woolf 1975: 267). This proliferation of essays, Woolf argues, has caused a lowering of standards of essay writing. She links this to the conditions of journalism in the twentieth century: namely, tighter deadlines and word limitations.

She looks particularly at the personal essay, and argues, in 'The Decay of Essay Writing', that the essay has become an excuse for the indulgence of egoism, 'under the decent veil of print' (Woolf 1986: 26). She is looking for the truly autobiographical essay, like Montaigne's for instance, but instead finds writers and journalists using the essay to show off, unwilling to look honestly at themselves. This, remember, was what Montaigne was advocating: a recognition of man's fallibility. In 'The Modern Essay', Woolf contrasts the intimacy and informality of the modern essay with nineteenth-century essays, in which 'Matthew Arnold was never to his readers Matt, nor Walter Pater affectionately abbreviated in a thousand homes to Wat' (Woolf 1975: 274). In the modern essay, she argues, rather than having a gospel to preach, essayists want to present themselves, 'simply and directly' (Woolf 1975: 274).

The modern journalistic essay

In the second half of the twentieth century, the essay form developed further, responding to changes in the ways in which we communicate with one another. Particularly in America, writers have combined fiction, journalism, cinematic documentary and biography to find new forms and subjects for the essay. We still continue to read essays in literary magazines such as the *London Review of Books* and the *Times Literary Supplement*, but the expansion of newspaper journalism has meant that there are more and more essays, in the form of feature articles and opinion pieces in the daily newspapers.

In 1960s America, a radically new form of essay emerged out of the world of journalism in magazines like *Rolling Stone*, *Esquire*, *Harper's* and the *New Yorker*. Writers such as Tom Wolfe, Truman Capote and Norman Mailer, among others, developed a form of journalistic writing which combined the essay, the short story, the anecdote, travel writing and the character sketch. Again, this new form was very much linked to historical, political and cultural changes which were taking place in 1960s America. Huge changes in social attitudes and behaviour gave rise to a new form of writing as a way of chronicling these changes. As Tom Wolfe wrote, the New Journalism had 'the whole crazed obscene uproarious Mammon-faced drug-soaked mau-mau lust-oozing Sixties in America all to themselves' (Wolfe 1973: 31).

The New Journalists' primary task was reportage, their essays were the results of exhaustive interviewing, note-taking and observing, but the ways in which they wrote about their findings are unique. Their essays do not rely on verbatim quoting, but instead recreate characters and settings through description, imagery, comedy and satire. Their essays are often written from the point of view of the interviewee, rather than the conventional journalistic perspective of the interviewer. The New Journalism, then, uses the techniques of realism, but this is combined with the modernity of the prose: its vibrancy, colloquialisms, and dramatic quality.

In the early 1960s, Tom Wolfe, author of *Bonfire of the Vanities*, was asked to do a news story on the custom car industry. He duly went along to the Hot Rod and Custom Car Show, and wrote a story which was published in *Esquire* called 'The Kandy-Kolored Tangerine-Flake Streamline Baby'. Here is its opening:

> Ten o'clock Sunday morning in the hills of North Carolina. Cars, miles of cars, in every direction, millions of cars, pastel cars, aqua green, aqua blue, aqua beige, aqua buff, aqua dawn, aqua dusk, aqua Malacca, Malacca lacquer, Cloud lavender, Assassin pink, Rake-a cheek raspberry, Nude Strand coral, Honest thrill orange, and Baby Fawn Lust cream colored cars are all going to the stock car races, and that old mothering North Carolina sun keeps exploding off the windshields.
>
> Seventeen thousand people, me included, all of us driving out Route 421, out to the stock car races at the North Wilkesboro Speedway, 17,000 going out to a five-eighths-mile stock car track with a Coca-Cola sign out front. This is not to say there is no preaching and shouting in the South this morning. There is preaching and shouting. Any of us can turn on the old automobile transistor radio and get all we want:
>
> 'They are greedy dogs. Yeah! They ride around in big cars. Unnh-hunh! And chase women. Yeah! And drink liquor. Unnh-hunh! And smoke cigars. Oh yes! And they are greedy dogs. Yeah! Unh-hunh! Oh yes! Amen!'
>
> (Wolfe 1982: 27)

The essay is about Junior Johnson, one of the fastest automobile racing drivers, but the opening of the piece sets the scene in North Carolina. The passage bombards the senses: the colour, sound and heat of the morning. The preacher's voice on the radio is dramatised rather than described, again, with the vitality so typical of New Journalism. Another trait of New Journalism is the use of satire and irony, as seen in the juxtaposition of the evangelist's condemnation of big cars and the car journey to the races. The colours of the cars grab the reader, through the inventiveness of the adjectives used to describe them. The scene described is not fiction, it is one that Wolfe really experienced, but we are given so much more than the bare facts: Wolfe uses language to bring the scene to life. New Journalism is perhaps the best example of the intersection between the essay and other genres and even media, such as the short story, the character sketch, and film.

ACTIVITY 5:

What follows is the opening of another Tom Wolfe essay from *Mauve Gloves and Madmen, Clutter and Vine.* Consider the following questions and write up your answers as a short report:

- Where does Wolfe position himself in the passage? What is his relationship to the well-known writer and what effect does this have?
- What techniques are used to make the passage so visual?
- How does Wolfe evoke 1970s America in the passage?
- How does Wolfe use appearance and fashion to tell us more about the well-known writer?
- How is irony used in the passage?

> The well-known American writer ... but perhaps it's best not to say exactly which well-known American writer ... they're a sensitive breed! The most ordinary comments they take personally! And why would the gentleman we're about to surprise be any exception? He's in his apartment, a seven-room apartment on Riverside Drive, on the West Side of Manhattan, in his study, seated at his desk. As we approach from the rear, we notice a bald spot on the crown of his head. It's about the size of a Sunshine Chip-a-Roo cookie, this bald spot, freckled and toasty brown. Gloriously suntanned, in fact. Around this bald spot swirls a corona of dark-brown hair that becomes quite thick by the time it completes its mad Byronic rush down the back over his turtleneck and out to the side in great bushes over his ears. He knows the days of covered ears are numbered, because that particular look has become somewhat Low Rent. When he was coming back from his father's funeral, half the salesmen lined up at O'Hare for the commuter flights, in their pajama-striped shirts and diamond-print double-knit suits, had groovy hair much like his. And to think that just six years ago such a hairdo seemed ... so defiant!

> (Wolfe 1982: 313)

ACTIVITY 6:

Write a 300-word introduction to a well-known public figure in the style of New Journalism.

The essay and racial politics

Throughout its history, the essay has been used for political purposes. James Baldwin (1924–87), an African-American novelist and essayist, published many well-known collections of essays on questions of race. *Notes of a Native Son* (1964) is one such collection. In the 'Autobiographical Notes' which open this volume, Baldwin asserts: 'One writes out of one thing only – one's own experience' (Baldwin 1995: 15). Here, we are back to Montaigne and his preface to his essays: the idea that the essay is an exploration of the self. Montaigne, and other writers, take for granted that this is a perfectly natural and realisable process. Baldwin's argument in his preface is that it is that very process of self-exploration which has been denied him. Racial discrimination has prevented him from writing openly about black experience: 'The difficulty then, for me, of being a Negro writer was the fact that I was, in effect, prohibited from examining my own experience too closely by the tremendous demands and the very real dangers of my social situation' (Baldwin 1995: 15). The essays which follow, which deal with his experience as an African-American in America and in Europe, constitute that self-examination, that reclaiming of identity, which has been denied him. 'I have not written about being a Negro at such length because I expect that to be my only subject, but only because it was the gate I had to unlock before I could hope to write about anything else' (Baldwin 1995: 15). The autobiographical element of Baldwin's essays, then, is a political statement in itself. The last essay in the collection, 'Stranger in the Village', demonstrates the movement between autobiography, or personal experience, and larger, more general, arguments. The personal is the political. The essay form allows this crossover. Here are the first and last paragraphs of the essay:

> From all available evidence no black man had ever set foot in this tiny Swiss village before I came. I was told before arriving that I would probably be a 'sight' for the village; I took this to mean that people of my complexion were rarely seen in Switzerland, and also that city people are always something of a 'sight' outside of the city. It did not occur to me – possibly because I am an American – that there could be people anywhere who had never seen a Negro.

> The time has come to realise that inter-racial drama acted out on the American continent has not only created a new black man, it has created a new white man, too. No road whatever will lead Americans back to the simplicity of this European village where white men still have the luxury of looking on me as a stranger. I am not, really, a stranger any longer for any American alive. One of the things that distinguishes Americans from other people is that no other people has ever been so deeply involved in the lives of black men, and vice versa. This fact faced, with all its implications, it can be seen that the history of the American Negro problem is not merely shameful, it is also something of an achievement. For even when the worst has been said, it must also be added that the perpetual challenge posed by this problem was always, somehow, perpetually met.

It is precisely this black–white experience which may prove of indispensable value to us in the world we face today. This world is white no longer, and it will never be white again.

(Baldwin 1995: 151 and 165)

ACTIVITY 7:

Analyse the movement between introduction and conclusion. How does Baldwin intertwine the personal and the general? Discuss the effectiveness of the first and final sentences of the essay. How would you describe Baldwin's prose style?

ACTIVITY 8:

Using the internet, find five to ten collections of essays by single authors written in the last five years. By using the titles, the book jacket descriptions and any on-line reviews available, demonstrate the range of subjects and styles of essay writing in the collections you have chosen.

ACTIVITY 9:

Find an essay/opinion piece in any contemporary newspaper or literary magazine. Analyse the effectiveness of the essayist's argument, use of evidence, style, register. How does the essay you have found differ from the extracts from other essays you have read in this chapter?

ACTIVITY 10:

Find an essay/opinion piece in a contemporary newspaper or literary magazine. Choose an appropriate subject and write an opening paragraph in imitation of the style and methods of your chosen essayist. Add a short commentary describing what you were trying to achieve.

Summary

Having looked at examples of a wide variety of essays, written at different times, for different purposes and using different techniques, we will now, for the rest of this book, focus on the academic essay. When you write academic essays you are presenting an argument on a particular subject, you are not writing a character sketch, an autobiographical monologue or a verse essay, and so academic essays follow certain conventions which we will look at in subsequent chapters. In this chapter we have covered the following topics:

- the essay in history: a genre which has responded to cultural change
- the variety of types of essays
- the variety of purposes in writing essays
- the variety of techniques used in essay writing.

This chapter has also introduced you to a variety of styles and to many examples of interesting and dynamic prose writers. This will help you in developing your own style within the conventions of the academic essay.

References

Bacon, Francis (1985) *The Essays*, ed. John Pitcher. Middlesex: Penguin.

Baldwin, James (1995) *Notes of a Native Son* [1964]. London: Penguin.

Cuddon, J.A. (1977) *A Dictionary of Literary Terms*. London: Andre Deutsch.

Dickens, Charles (1981) *Our Mutual Friend* [1864–65]. Oxford: Oxford University Press.

Gross, John (ed.) (1991) *The Oxford Book of Essays*. Oxford: Oxford University Press.

Lukács, Georg (1974) *Soul and Form*, trans. Anna Bostock. London: Merlin Press.

Montaigne, Michel de (1965) *The Complete Essays of Montaigne*, trans. Donald M. Frame. Stanford: Stanford University Press.

Obaldia, Claire de (1995) *The Essayistic Spirit*. Oxford: Clarendon Press.

Pater, Walter (1910) *Plato and Platonism*. London: Macmillan.

Pope, Alexander (1972) *Selected Poetry and Prose*, ed. William K. Wimsatt. New York: Holt, Rinehart and Winston.

Wolfe, Tom (1973) *The New Journalism*. New York: Harper and Row.

Wolfe, Tom (1982) *The Purple Decades*. New York: Farrar Straus Giroux.

Woolf, Virginia (1975) *The Common Reader. First Series*. London: Hogarth Press.

Woolf, Virginia (1986) *The Essays of Virginia Woolf, Vol. I*, ed. Andrew McNeillie. London: Hogarth Press.

Style and voice in academic writing

Rebecca Stott

I n the last chapter we looked at the history of the essay as a genre. In this chapter we shall be looking at the conventions of the academic essay and at the variety of style and voice in academic writing. We shall argue that although there are certain conventions of academic essay writing, what we might call a house style, nonetheless for writers working within these expectations and conventions there are as many different kinds of voice as there are writers. We will also suggest ways in which you can improve your own writing style and ensure that you have a distinctive and confident voice in writing.

Acquiring a good style in writing is not easy, whatever form of writing you are trying to produce. All the writers whom we quote in this book have honed their writing abilities through practice. Most of them have probably been writing every day for decades. If you were to ask them about the development of their style, they would probably say that the way they write now is very different from the way they wrote when they were just starting out as writers. The daily business of the writer is a struggle with language: the search for the right word, the right place in the sentence, the right combination of words to create a language that is vital rather than jaded. Redrafting is at the heart of all effective writing, not just fiction. For writers of civil service documents or video manuals, this means that finding the right word is not just pedantry but absolutely vital, because without it meaning can become ambiguous, resulting in misunderstandings, wasted time and frustration. Words must be used like precision tools.

Many writers and academics have written about the importance of developing a strong voice in academic writing. Here is Nicole Ward-Jouve on taking risks in writing in an extract from her book *White Woman Speak with Forked Tongue: Criticism as Autobiography*:

Thinking means putting everything on the line, taking risks, writerly risks, finding out what the actual odds are, not sheltering behind a pretend and in any case fallacious and transparent objectivity. Only when it actually thinks is criticism ever a form of writing. Only then is it a total commitment to language, the way a joiner who makes a table will choose the best wood he or she can get, attempt to serve the wood well, use his or her skill to best effect, invest everything, body and knowledge, into what the old Compagnons used to call a masterpiece (which could also be a mistresspiece) . . .

The only way in which you can be genuinely stimulated and fed by discourses you admire or find congenial is if you dare conquer a voice of your own.

. . . however different your craft and your skills and your object, you are still in the same business as the artists themselves.

(Ward-Jouve 1991: 9–11)

For Nicole Ward-Jouve, writing academic essays is a craft just as writing fiction is a craft. You have to learn how to do it and you have to care about doing it. She holds this view in part because she is both an academic and a novelist, and because although she changes what she does when she shifts from being an academic writer to being a novelist and back again, she is still looking for finely crafted sentences and an integrity of voice.

Seamus Heaney is also a writer who writes in a number of different forms. He is a Nobel Prize-winning poet and a respected writer of academic essays on poetry, edited into two collections called *Government of the Tongue* and *Preoccupations*. In an essay in the second volume called 'Feeling into Words', he writes about the time when, as a young poet, he began to find his own voice, not through writing constantly, but through reading and listening for sounds and rhythms:

I think that the discovery of a way of writing that is natural and adequate to your sensibility depends on the recovery of the essential quick which Solzhenitzyn's technicians were trying to pin down. This is the absolute register to which your proper music has to be tuned.

How, then, do you find it? In practice, you hear it coming from somebody else, you hear something in another writer's sounds that flows in through your ear and enters the echo-chamber of your head and delights your whole nervous system in such a way that your reaction will be, 'Ah, I wish I had said that, in that particular way.' This other writer, in fact, has spoken something essential to you, something you recognise instinctively as a true sounding of aspects of yourself and your experience. And your first steps as a writer will be to imitate, consciously or unconsciously, those sounds that flowed in, that in-fluence.

(Heaney 1980: 44–5)

So the first step for Seamus Heaney, learning to write poetry, was the imitation of the sounds in other people's writing that sounded true to his own experience and self. This is how many people begin. In fact it's how we all begin – as children – to find our own voice through imitating the babble of adult voices we hear around us. Imitation is a necessary part of the process of learning to speak in different registers and within different conventions. Gradually we learn to become flexible and adaptable to different situations and find our own way of writing because if we are only ever able to imitate the voices of others we will not inspire confidence. Teenagers, for instance, often run into trouble with the way that they speak or write because they cannot quite control the growing number of registers they have begun to acquire or are not quite able to judge when one is appropriate or inappropriate.

Academic register and conventions

What are the conventions of contemporary academic writing – the essays that students write in higher education and the essays that academics write for journals or collections of essays? We should address these before we go any further in order to acknowledge the huge variation of style that academic writers achieve within these conventions. What do we, as readers, expect from academic writing? What do we, as writers, expect from academic writing?

Seriousness of approach

This speaks for itself. We expect a seriousness in the way the writer addresses the issue and a seriousness in the voice. This doesn't mean that humour is inappropriate, but seriousness will be paramount. Flippancy, colloquialism, and phrases like 'you know what I mean' or 'and all that stuff' will sound out of place. On the other hand this seriousness of approach doesn't mean that you have to sound earnest all the time.

A certain formality of register

This is in keeping with the seriousness of tone and approach. The register will be formal, not colloquial. It will reflect the considered and measured thought-processes that will be going on. It treats the reader as if they were an interested and informed acquaintance, but not a best-mate.

Consistency of register

We expect the formal register to be consistent throughout the essay. Register-slippage and contrast can be very effective in comic writing (the writer suddenly becomes intimate or very pompous and keeps shifting from one voice to another throughout the writing in order to create parody or a sense of the absurd) but is inappropriate in academic writing. It is also very difficult to achieve for those only beginning to write.

Objectivity of tone

Because the writer is engaged in persuasion, argument and assessment, readers assume that the writer will try to be objective and neutral. We would be surprised for instance to read: 'Keith Samuels reveals his own stupidity when he argues in *Nineteenth-Century Lives* that Elizabeth Barrett Browning's poetry was influenced by her husband'. The register here is formal enough, but the jibe of stupidity does not sound neutral and object-ive. Generally we expect academic essays to argue, not to abuse or accuse.

Cautiousness about the way claims are made

Objectivity will be conveyed in this cautiousness or what is called in lin-guistics 'modality'. Its flavour can be caught in phrases such as 'it could be said that' or 'certain critics have claimed that' or 'this might lead us to the interpretation that'.

Reasoned, analytical and logical thought-processes

If we are going to be persuaded by the writer, if we are going to accept the case that is being made, we will expect the writer to be analytical and to take us through the issues in a sequential and logical way and to explain the decisions as they are made. Once again linking sentences are crucial here, such as: 'I have shown how George Eliot's assumption of a pseudonym affected her prose style in her early journalism, but it remains to be shown how this pseudonym may have affected her prose style in fiction'.

Concern with argument and evidence

We will usually expect the writer to be careful to provide evidence for each claim made as the essay progresses and for that evidence to be properly referenced. Evidence is likely to be drawn from a variety of appropriate sources, including primary texts and a range of secondary texts which might include for instance reference books and works of secondary criticism.

ACTIVITY 1:

Do you agree with our list of features of academic writing? Are there any you would add or change?

ACTIVITY 2:

Read the following three extracts from academic essays by Frederic Jameson, Elaine Showalter and Tony Tanner and consider the following questions:

- Do the extracts meet the expectations and conventions of academic writing as we have outlined them above?
- How do they convey a sense of objectivity?
- How do they make you feel confident that they know their subjects?
- How would you describe the differences in the way that they write?
- What words would you use to differentiate their prose styles or voices?
- Which do you prefer to read and why?

Extract from an essay by Frederic Jameson on postmodernism

Now I must try very rapidly in conclusion to characterise the relationship of cultural production of this kind to social life in this country today. This will also be the moment to address the principal objection to concepts of postmodernism of the type I have sketched here: namely that all the features we have enumerated are not new at all but abundantly characterised modernism proper or what I call high modernism. Was not Thomas Mann, after all, interested in the idea of pastiche, and are not certain chapters of *Ulysses* its most obvious realisation? Can Flaubert, Mallarmé and Gertrude Stein not be included in an account of postmodernist temporality? What is so new about all of this? Do we really need the concept of *post*modernism?

(Jameson 1988: 26)

Opening paragraph from Elaine Showalter's Introduction to *Daughters of Decadence: Women Writers of the Fin-De-Siècle*, Virago, 1993

When we think of the literature of the *fin-de-siècle*, the writers who come most readily to mind are men, whether they are the aesthetes and decadents who drank absinthe on the Wilde side, or strolled down Piccadilly with lilies in their hands; the adventurers who described the search for King Solomon's Mines or the journey to the exotic heart of darkness; the essayists who contemplated modern life from the windows of the Saville Club or the visionaries who championed sexual freedom, the celebrated artists of the 1890s do not include women. Yet for feminist thinkers and writers, the *fin-de-siècle* was also a period of exploration and experiment. Recalling the first London production of Ibsen's *A Doll's House* in 1889, Edith Lees described how women in the audience, including Olive Schreiner and Eleanor Marx, lingered after the play, 'breathless with excitement…We were restive and impetuous and almost savage in our arguments. This was either the end of the world or the beginning of a new world for women. What did it mean? Was there hope or despair in the banging of that door? Was it life or death for women? Was it joy or sorrow for men? Was it revelation or disaster?'

(Showalter 1993: vi)

Opening paragraph from Tony Tanner's Introduction to the Penguin edition of Jane Austen's *Mansfield Park*

Many great novels concern themselves with characters whose place in society is not fixed or assured. Foundlings, orphans, outsiders, people moving from one country to another, people moving from one class to another, those who have to create the shape of their lives as they go along, or those who find themselves in movements or changes over which they only have partial control – such people are common frequenters of the novel. Whether you think of Tom Jones, or Julien Sorel (in *Le Rouge et le noir*), or Becky Sharpe (in *Vanity Fair*), or Jude Fawley (in *Jude the Obscure*), or Isabel Archer (in *Portrait of a Lady*), or Paul Morel (in *Sons and Lovers*), or even of Saul Bellow's Augie March, these are all characters who at the start of the novel are not defined or fulfilled by their status or locality or position. They cannot and do not take their place in society for granted, and they end up – whether happily or otherwise – with a different social identity. In the course of such novels there has been choice and change. The characters might have their virtue ultimately rewarded, like Tom Jones; or their ambitions thwarted, like Jude; or they may be imprisoned by the hateful consequences of their own errors, like Isabel Archer. In every case we can generally say that we are watching the initially undefined and uncommitted self having to take on definition through what happens to it in society. The self may be able to choose what happens, it may simply permit it, or it may have to suffer it: its quest for definition may entail true discovery of the self, and it may finally precipitate destruction of the self. But whatever else happens to these characters, they have moved. They are not where they were; they are not what they were. And so it is with Fanny Price, the heroine of *Mansfield Park*.

(Tanner 1966: 7)

ACTIVITY 3:

Read the following extract from a piece of critical writing about the American poet Walt Whitman, written by the novelist, poet and artist D.H. Lawrence and first published in 1924. Lawrence's collection of essays on American literature has remained in print since then and is generally well-regarded by American scholars because, despite the (refreshing!)

eccentricity of Lawrence's style, the essays are nonetheless serious critical engagements with the writing. They have a great deal to say that is original and incisive.

I am he that aches with amorous love:
Does the earth gravitate, does not all matter, aching, attract all matter?
So the body of me to all I meet or know.
(Walt Whitman, 1867)

> I AM HE THAT ACHES WITH AMOROUS LOVE.
> What do you make of that? I AM HE THAT ACHES. First generalisation. First uncomfortable universalisation. WITH AMOROUS LOVE! Oh God! Better a bellyache. A bellyache is at least specific. But the ACHE OF AMOROUS LOVE!
> Think of having that under your skin. All that!
> I AM HE THAT ACHES WITH AMOROUS LOVE.
> Walter, leave off. You are not HE. You are just a limited Walter. And your ache doesn't include all Amorous Love, by any means. If you ache you only ache with a small bit of amorous love, and there's so much more stays outside the cover of your ache, that you might be a bit milder about it.
> I AM HE THAT ACHES WITH AMOROUS LOVE.
> CHUFF! CHUFF! CHUFF!
> CHE-CHU-CHU-CHU-CHUFF!
> Reminds one of a steam-engine. A locomotive. They're the only things that seem to me to ache with amorous love. All that steam inside them. Forty-million foot pounds pressure. The ache of AMOROUS LOVE. Steam-pressure. CHUFF!
> An ordinary man aches with love for Belinda, or his Native Land, or the Ocean, of the Stars, of the Oversoul: if he feels that an ache is in the fashion.
> It takes a steam-engine to ache with AMOROUS LOVE. All of it.
> Walt was really too superhuman. The danger of the superman is that he is mechanical.
> They talk of his 'splendid animality'. Well, he'd got it on the brain, if that's the place for animality.

(Lawrence 1955: 393)

Consider the following questions and write up your answers as a short report:

- What surprises you about the way Lawrence writes here?
- How much of that surprise is due to your expectations about what critical writing should be like?
- What specific expectations about academic writing does Lawrence break with in this extract?
- What do you like/dislike about it and why?
- Summarise Lawrence's main claim from this extract.
- How does Lawrence show his authority on the subject?
- Does Lawrence convey objectivity?
- What words would you use to describe his prose style or voice?
- Why is it that Lawrence can publish critical work of this kind?

ACTIVITY 4:

Rewrite this passage retaining Lawrence's key ideas about Whitman's poetry but expressing them in a more conventional academic register. What has been gained and/or lost in the transposition? Or write an opening paragraph to a recent academic essay question you have answered in the style of Lawrence's essay above.

ACTIVITY 5:

Read the following passage from a book called *Literary Theory: An Introduction* by Terry Eagleton. Eagleton has just provided a reading of D.H. Lawrence's *Sons and Lovers* to show how it is possible to read the novel in its social context and to provide a psychoanalytical reading of the novel at the same time. He argues from this that these two kinds of readings can actually complement each other.

> In reading *Sons and Lovers* with an eye to these aspects of the novel, we are constructing what may be called a 'sub-text' for the work – a text which runs within it, visible at certain 'symptomatic' points of ambiguity, evasion or overemphasis, and which we as readers are able to 'write' even if the novel itself does not. All literary works contain one or more such sub-texts, and there is a sense in which they may be spoken of as the 'unconscious' of the work itself. The work's insights, as with all writing, are deeply related to its blindnesses: what it does not say, and how it does not say it, may be as important as what it does say, and how it does not say it, may be as important as what it articulates; what seems absent, marginal or ambivalent about it may provide a central clue to its meaning. We are not simply rejecting or inverting 'what the novel says', arguing, for example, that Morel is the real hero and his wife the villain. Paul's viewpoint is not simply valid: his mother is indeed an incomparably richer source of sympathy than his father. We are looking rather at what such statements must inevitably silence or suppress, examining the ways in which the novel is not quite identical with itself. Psychoanalytical criticism, in other words, can do more than hunt for phallic symbols: it can tell us something about how literary texts are actually formed, and reveal something of the meaning of that formation.
>
> (Eagleton 1983: 179)

Now consider the following questions:

- How would you describe the way Eagleton writes?
- What do you like/dislike about his style and voice, and why?
- Are there any techniques he uses that you think are particularly effective for expository writing of this kind?

ACTIVITY 6:

Write a version of Eagleton's paragraph in your own voice.

Some suggestions for improving style in academic writing

So far in this chapter we have identified some of the conventions of academic writing and looked at the wide range of voice and style it is possible to achieve within these conventions. As I said earlier in the chapter, it is not possible to teach style, as everyone needs to develop their own ways of writing, but good writers generally make sure they practice their skills, are prepared to draft and redraft their work until it is as polished as it can be, and learn techniques and skills from other writers they admire.

Here are some guidelines for improving style; they can be found in most style manuals, but we have adapted them for the novice academic writer:

- Avoid passive constructions where possible.
- Try to develop a direct, clear style.
- Say what you think and why you think it but always justify your arguments and opinions.
- Use rhetorical questions from time to time to refocus your argument.
- Avoid unnecessary jargon (you will need to use some technical terms). If you have to use jargon, explain what you mean by it.
- Cut out deadwood in the editing stage.
- State clearly what your questions are and when appropriate state clearly what you think you have discovered.
- Spend time proof-reading and editing your work in order to clarify your arguments and to improve your prose style.
- Vary sentence length and format so that the writing is never monotonous in its rhythms.
- Use your own words – don't parrot the words of academics if they are not words you would use comfortably.
- Learn from writers you admire.

ACTIVITY 7:

Choose a piece of writing from a critic whose writing style you admire. What is it about this style that makes you want to read more? What features and techniques can you incorporate into your own writing?

ACTIVITY 8:

Take a piece of your own recent essay writing. Analyse its style in terms of the conventions of academic writing we identified earlier in this chapter. Does it meet all those expectations? Identify the characteristics of your own style in the light of the observations we have made in this chapter. What words would you use to describe it? Do you have a voice that you think is recognisably yours? If not, why not? Do you feel that you write in your own academic voice or borrow the academic voices of others? What is good/less good about your style? What can you do to improve it?

Rewrite a paragraph of your essay in order to implement the changes you think are necessary.

ACTIVITY 9:

Read the range of introductions to student essays below. Some are answers to questions set by tutors and some are topics defined by the students themselves. Consider the following questions:

- What voices are you drawn to and why?
- What voices do you find jarring and why?
- What strategies for writing engage you as the reader and why?
- Which prose style would you wish to emulate?
- Which is closest to your own style?
- What are the strengths and weaknesses of each writing style?

1. How useful is the term 'realism' in describing the literature of the nineteenth century?

Before attempting to determine the usefulness of the term 'realism' it is perhaps expedient to explore its inherent problems. Probably the primary difficulty, and the one which generates many lesser ones, is that the meaning of 'realism' is in constant flux and as such is always culturally relative. It is perhaps only an art arising from a common culture and shared tradition which can aspire towards an aesthetic of realism. Diverse belief systems, cultural norms and moral perspectives which emerge from multiple ethnic and ideological sources destabilise the concept of realism, rendering it relative and naive. Use of the term realism seems to require consensus, yet modern and post-modern views of the world hold that the only current consensus is that there is no consensus. The use of the term in literary criticism cannot be separated from the philosophical question of what constitutes reality itself, and the inevitable epistemological question which follows, that of how can we know? These are metaphysical questions which are endlessly debatable but which cannot easily be shelved, or put aside, in relation to the literature of the nineteenth century.

2. Fleshliness and masculinity in Algernon Swinburne's 'Anactoria'.

The Fleshly School of Poets, writing in the 1860s and 1870s, reacted to and were an expression of the deep anxieties that surrounded the crisis of gender and in particular the crisis of masculinity in Victorian England towards the end of the nineteenth century. Their poetry focused on illicit and indulgent sexual and emotional relations and reworked defined absolutes of gender and beauty. By making language achieve different ends they forced a redefinition of gender that would replace the prescribed gender norms of Victorian culture. Masculinity was re-envisaged by breaking down gender boundaries and placing emphasis on deviant sexuality and sexual desire found in looking at the borderlines of gender. In so doing they forced a new language and discourse for the forbidden topic of sexual attraction and male and female relations.

3. The use of architecture as a narrative structuring device in the novels of Charlotte Brontë.

It might be said that the pilgrimages of Charlotte Brontë's heroines are not so much interior because they represent the incarceration of women in the home in Victorian society, but because, in the increasingly industrialised world of Victorian England, the only pilgrimages possible are urban ones. Brontë's novels sometimes create a strange foreshadowing of the suffocating interiors of the early twentieth-century writer Franz Kafka, in which doors stick and characters become increasingly buried in over-heated urban labyrinths and maze-like institutions. But perhaps Brontë's world offers its heroines more opportunities than the paranoid world of Kafka, for the corridors are long and the doors are many and adventures and experiences of a million kinds lie behind them all.

4. Explore the difficulties of producing a critical account of novels such as *Tristram Shandy* and *Orlando* which challenged the very definitions and classifications of literary criticism.

Occasionally an item of creative writing falls into the hands of a literary critic and produces expressions of alarm, perhaps not dissimilar to those generated by a hot chestnut falling into the lap of an improperly dressed cleric (Sterne 1985: 315–21). Two such works have been *Tristram Shandy* and *Orlando*; the alarm arises from their seeming unaccountability. Some reference to the development of the novel genre is expedient to an exploration of why these works create such difficulties. In his book *The Rise of the Novel*, Ian Watt states that the emergence of the novel, during the eighteenth century, coincided with radical changes in philosophy, especially its relinquishing of a definition of reality that had been located in abstract universals (Watt 1987: 9), in favour of one based on individual experience.

5. 'Femininity is a cultural construct: one isn't born a woman, one becomes one' (Simone de Beauvoir). A study of representations of femininity in Christina Rossetti's 'Goblin Market'.

Who shall measure the heat and violence of the poet's heart when caught and tangled in a woman's body?

(Virginia Woolf)

This essay will attempt to illustrate the continuously shifting constructs of femininity embedded in Christina Rossetti's 'Goblin Market'. It will explore the relationship between the extrinsic and visibly Victorian 'cultural construct' of femininity with this poetess's intrinsic ability, within this patriarchal order, to remould and re-create through the text a variety of mutable and multi-faceted feminine identities. This essay will propose that 'the heat and violence of the poet's heart when caught and tangled in a woman's body' ignites the 'productive tensions between the political and the aesthetic, between history and text' (Huyssen in Leighton 1996: 6), whilst simultaneously allowing Rossetti, as a female poet, an opportunity to discover through her creativity a rich diversity of alternative feminine constructs.

6. 'The most powerful war poetry is retrospective and reflective.' Discuss.

Is it important to see the whole picture, including the outcome of the First World War, in order to write profoundly on the subject? Is it important that the poet be abstracted from the terrible situation, in possession of all the facts so that his poetry is more objective? Does accuracy necessarily constitute powerful poetry? Indeed, it may be argued that the poetry of Owen and Sassoon, of the period 1914–18, is desperately powerful and moving for the very fact that it is full of uncertainty, and that their total involvement with death, killing, trenches and mud meant that they could not see past that horror and take a broader view of events. The strength of the poetry written between 1914 and 1918 works on two levels, firstly through the compassion with which Owen writes, and secondly through Sassoon's anger, frustration and in some cases contempt for those in positions of influence and authority, which manifest themselves in the form of satire.

7. Starting from a discussion of the details in the given article, and the issues it raises, consider the relative effectiveness of standard and non-standard English as means of communication. Refer to a range of examples.

The article is discussing the advantages and the usage of non-standard English in a particular environment. However, there are also several underlying issues which can be seen as important in an examination of the relative effectiveness of such language and the comparable use of Standard English. Firstly a consideration of the article itself is required in order to achieve an understanding of the issues amplified.

> **8. 'Religious and theological argument was inseparable from every human concern whether political or personal in this period.' Discuss.**
>
> In 1625 John Milton was admitted to Christ's College, Cambridge, where he completed a B.A. and proceeded to his M.A. in 1632. One year later Dr William Laud was appointed Archbishop of Canterbury. Although he had anticipated a life in the service of the Church, nevertheless having completed his education, Milton felt he could not take orders in a Church of which Archbishop Laud had the direction. Although superficially the two men differ only in matters of religion, I believe the underlying conflict of ideas between these two individuals characterises the way in which theological argument, political and personal life became entangled during the period.

ACTIVITY 10:

Choose the extract above which you feel has the most awkward prose style. Rewrite it in a voice that is more natural to you. Try to remember the guidelines for effective writing outlined in this chapter. Redraft it as many times as you can in the time available.

Summary

In this chapter we have looked at:

- conventions of academic writing
- varieties of voice and style achieved within these conventions
- ways in which you can improve your own academic writing style.

References

Eagleton, Terry (1983) *Literary Theory: An Introduction*. Oxford: Blackwell.

Heaney, Seamus (1980) 'Feeling into Words' in *Preoccupations: Selected Prose 1968–1978*. London: Faber and Faber.

Jameson, Frederic (1988) 'Postmodernism and Consumer Society' in E. Ann Kaplan (ed.), *Postmodernism and its Discontents*. London: Verso.

Lawrence, D.H. (1955) 'Walt Whitman' in *Selected Literary Criticism*. London: Heinemann. First published in 1924 as *Studies in Classical American Literature*.

Leighton, Angela (ed.) (1996) *Victorian Women Poets: A Critical Reader*. Oxford: Blackwell.

Showalter, Elaine (1993) *Daughters of Decadence: Women Writers of the Fin-De-Siècle*. London: Virago.

Sterne, Lawrence (1985) *The Life and Opinions of Tristram Shandy Gentleman*. Harmondsworth: Penguin.

Tanner, Tony (1966) Introduction to Jane Austen, *Mansfield Park*. Harmondsworth:
Penguin.

Ward-Jouve, Nicole (1991) *White Woman Speaks with Forked Tongue: Criticism as
Autobiography*. London: Routledge.

Watt, Ian (1987) *The Rise of the Novel: Studies in Defoe, Richardson and Fielding*. London:
Hogarth.

The essay writing process

Rebecca Stott

I n this chapter we will examine the essay writing process from defining the case to be made, brainstorming, planning, structuring, collecting evidence, to the final stages of editing and proof-reading. The exercises will give you the opportunity to practice the *first stages* of this process – brainstorming and planning (in rhetorical terms 'inventio' and 'dispositio').

Before we move on to consider the creative processes behind the production of a good academic essay, we should first consider what makes a good essay. So often students do not see other students' essays and may never set eyes on a first-class essay unless they are able to produce one themselves. We thought the best person to ask would be a tutor, someone who sees hundreds of essays a year and who has become skilled in making minute decisions and adjudicating about borderlines. The following is an interview with a tutor about the marking process.

What makes a good essay? A student interviews a lecturer

What kind of essays do you mark?
Mostly undergraduate English literature essays but also M.A. essays and occasionally I examine doctorates here and at other universities. I guess I must mark as many as 200 undergraduate essays a year, most of them with a word limit of 3,000 words. A few of these essays will be on a subject that the student has chosen, but mostly they are answers to a question or instruction set by us – you know, essays of the 'explore', 'discuss' or 'analyse' kind.

Oh, yes, we've had plenty of those . . . What would you say are the essential features of an academic essay?

What I have to keep reminding my students, particularly in the first year when they have been used to writing 'A' level essays, is that an academic essay is fundamentally an *argument*. That's not always the case, as sometimes you'll be asked to produce different kinds of written work for assessment purposes (a review, or a logbook, or even a piece of creative writing), but when you're asked for an essay you should think in terms of producing an argument.

The problem with so many essays is that there's loads of information but little or no argument. It's the difference between knowledge-telling and knowledge-transformation. Knowledge-telling is the regurgitation of knowledge in an essay. But knowledge-transformation is what's crucial: the ability to manipulate that basic, raw material in order to make a convincing argument. Very often I find myself reading knowledge-telling essays that demonstrate that the student knows the material, even that they've undertaken days of research, but these essays don't demonstrate the knowledge-transformation required to make an argument. The student is regurgitating either lecture materials or critical interpretations gleaned from critical texts or even plot summaries. The essay is therefore descriptive but not analytical. It's more like a summary or paraphrase.

What are you looking for as you begin reading?

The first thing I look for is evidence that the student has engaged with the question right from the start and is beginning to formulate an argument. The introduction is very important here. I'm looking to see that the dialogue with the question has begun. I'm also looking for a context. I want the student to tell me why his or her approach to the question is interesting and important. Sometimes the context will be historical or sociological or philosophical or sometimes the student will need to tell me that there's been a lot of debate in this area and explain why. I'm looking for focus, for a voice that I feel confident with and not bored by – someone who knows the area and is going to take me round the issues in an objective, informed and interesting way.

What are the things that make you critical in reading essays? Mistakes, bad referencing, poor handwriting?

Personally, I have a passionate aversion to unsubstantiated generalisations. You know – when someone opens a paragraph with a sentence like 'In the nineteenth century women thought . . .'. I always feel like saying in response: 'which women? *All* of them?' Because there were millions of women who lived in the nineteenth century and you simply can't lump them all into one group and say they all thought the same thing. We are trying to encourage students to be precise, subtle and careful in their thinking, and generalisations of that kind simply don't have a place in academic work.

I have a friend who has to restrain himself from writing 'nonsense' in the margin when he reads such claims.

I also find that in some essays the student is offering up lots of good material but without an argument and without answering the question – the knowledge-telling approach. Those are the descriptive essays and I want to say 'don't just tell me what happens, analyse it, give me an argument, a point of view'.

Punctuation and spelling errors also preoccupy me as I read. When there are lots and lots of errors you suspect that the student doesn't really care about it or they've rushed it in the last stages. I want to see that the student has given the essay as much care and attention as I am giving it. I want to see that they have taken the business seriously.

What makes a first-class essay and can you tell me how to write one!?
How to write a first-class essay . . . ? Oh, I wish it was as easy as that. There are so many different ways of writing one – which is why I can't give you the magic formula. Everyone has slightly different strengths and ways of writing. That's what makes it so interesting. One first-class essay might be highly theoretical, philosophical and conceptually sophisticated and another might be made up of a series of close readings of poems which offer a fresh interpretation of the poetry with very little theoretical context.

I have a rule of thumb for first-class essays and this is that most of them make me want to keep a copy for myself (and I do keep a file of xeroxes of first-class essays). Usually I will want to keep a copy because the essay has surprised me or made me think slightly differently about the subject or presented the material in a new way. They are always well-written, confidently expressed and have an originality that makes them great to read. They will have a clear argument that answers the question and they will use good evidence to back up all their main points.

How would you describe the very worst essays you see – the ones you fail or give very low pass marks to?
The essays I fail have usually gone very wrong in some way. They will usually make very little sense, be poorly expressed, lack coherence and sequence, and will be full of errors in grammar, punctuation and spelling. They are unlikely to engage with the question in any way and will probably be full of plot summary and verbose, undirected writing as padding. You know – lots of waffle. The essays that pass, but which only just make it, will probably consider the question in some way but lack any argument and make little reference to the text.

. . . the knowledge-telling approach?
Precisely. They're also likely to be full of unsubstantiated generalisations, repetitions and plot summary, and will probably also be inadequately edited and proof-read.

Where do you feel students throw most marks away?
Proof-reading and editing. Most students don't spend enough time on this. Sometimes you suspect that the student hasn't bothered reading it through at all when there are lots of mistakes, and the paragraphs don't hold together and it's all too verbose. When I correct mistakes of punctuation and spelling or suggest alterations such as a new paragraph here and a sentence or two taken out there, I feel that the student should have done this in the final draft stage, not me. When expression is poor, too, that is usually a result of inadequate editing. You feel that if only the student had taken an hour or two to read the essay aloud to him/herself they would be able to find more direct and fluent ways of saying what they want to say. Editing and proof-reading are not the final icing on the cake, as some people think. They are absolutely crucial because it's only at this stage that the student can see that the argument hangs together and makes sense, has a sequence and is well-expressed. Editing is both difficult and important.

I always hand-write my essays. How important is presentation?
Very important, because it tells the tutor how seriously the student has taken the essay. If the student has rushed the final draft it will be very visible not only because they've not proof-read properly, but because the format is inconsistent and the references incomplete. It gives a lot away. It is possible to get high marks with a poorly presented essay, though. I've given first-class marks very occasionally to essays which have been well-written, original, carefully structured and argued, but which have been badly presented because of almost illegible handwriting. But it's always a struggle with that kind of essay because the presentation becomes an obstacle to the tutor's pleasure in the ideas themselves. The carefully word-processed essay with wide margins, clear paragraphs, indented quotes and full references makes such a good impression right from the start and shows that the student has taken the work seriously. So the handwriting question depends a lot on what kind of handwriting you've got.

Can you judge an essay just by looking at it?
In some ways, yes. Some problems with essays are very *visible*. I mean, when people have a problem with structuring you can usually *see* it before you read it. Paragraphs will usually be very short, sometimes only one sentence, and the look on the page is of fragmentation, like a piece of shattered glass. These are scatter-gun essays. They are usually rushed, with ideas expressed randomly, not connected with each other. There are other kinds of essays that have structuring problems that are less acute but where the structure seems fragile in some way. Often you find that paragraphs have been started in random places because the writer doesn't really know the main point of this particular paragraph. This is usually because the student is finding their way as they go rather than starting with a plan. It's a fault in the planning stage.

If you are not sure about an essay – say it is borderline 2.1/2.2 – how do you make your final decision?

I go back over the essay paying particular attention to the places where I have put ticks in the margin and to the beginning and ending where I would expect the argument to be addressed directly. I also ask myself 'what is the proportion of analysis to description'. This is a good question to ask because it is possible for a very descriptive essay to answer the question in a round-about way. Generally though, if the essay is more descriptive than it is analytical it will get a 2.2. mark at the very most. If the essay has a good argument the quality of the argument will determine what mark it gets in the 2.1. range.

How can students improve their essays?

This is one of the most satisfying parts of teaching at university level – seeing students learn to write. I've taught students who have come to university with very poor writing skills. One student in particular I remember failed a number of essays in her first term. She was trying hard, doing all the right reading and research but her expression, punctuation, spelling and grammar were all so poor that she simply couldn't express the good ideas she had. She realised she had a problem and she took it seriously. She thought about the comments her tutors had made and went to see them to ask them to explain in more detail what was wrong with her work. She bought herself teach-yourself books on grammar and punctuation. She began to write plans for her essays. She spent hours and hours editing her work, checking for mistakes and polishing up the arguments and the expression. She kept going back to see her tutors for additional feedback. By the end of her first year her essays were of low 2.2. level. By the end of her second year she was getting 2.1 marks consistently and by the end of her third year she had gained two first-class marks. Her writing at the end of her degree course was concise, elegant, expressive and a pleasure to read. She is now a secondary school teacher and has a particular responsibility in the school for overseeing writing skills.

(interview conducted by J. Morrish)

ACTIVITY 1:

Either working alone or in groups, devise a list of five questions which you would like to ask a lecturer about academic essays. These might be modelled on the questions the student above has asked or may be completely different. Find a lecturer in a department other than your own (but which assesses its students largely through essay writing) and interview him/her with your questions. Analyse the answers, paying particular attention to any differences of opinion or emphasis between your chosen lecturer and the lecturer we have interviewed in this chapter. If there are major differences, how much can these differences of opinion be explained by the differences between the disciplines?

Behind the scenes: the essay writing process

The next stage of this chapter is to consider the *process* of writing, to take a look behind the scenes to show how students reach that point of handing in what will be assessed as a good essay. We have considered the question 'what is a good essay?' and now we shall ask 'how is a good essay *made*?' This is a difficult question to answer as the creative processes behind essay writing are complex and often invisible. Not everyone follows the same stages in writing every single essay. Sometimes one stage will take much longer for one piece of work than for another. However, there have been a number of researchers who have looked at the practice of writing to see if expert writers share common activities in producing academic writing (see Grabe and Kaplan 1996) and we have tried to base our guide to the processes of essay writing on that research and on our own research into the practices that good writers follow in writing. The following guide should be seen as a kind of overview – not as a list of rules, but rather as a way to help you think about the *processes* of writing rather than merely the end-product. Once we have looked at the various stages in brief we will focus in more detail on each during this chapter and over the following chapters of the book.

1. Thinking about the question

Decide on your objective. What are you trying to prove? If you are answering a question, think over the wording of the question, pull it apart, analyse it, use a dictionary. Look out for key words – these help you focus on what the requirements are. Be sure you understand any specialist terms in the instructions. The time you spend clarifying the meaning of the question is time well spent. It will stop you researching the wrong information, you will focus on the topic areas intended by the marker, and you will gain better marks. If you are writing your own title, make sure it gives the reader a clear indication of your objective and of the parameters of your topic.

2. Brainstorming

Some people like to use a spider diagram at this stage which helps them map out all the connections between the various parts of ideas. Don't worry about producing too much material at this stage. Jot down all the ideas and questions you can think of in relation to the topic. Try to think about or find counter-arguments as well as your own arguments so that you are able to think *round* a subject and see it from as many different sides as possible. You will be able to select the more relevant and better-quality ideas in the next stage. At this stage you will also identify what areas you will need to research. What do you need to know or find out before you can argue your case well?

3. Gathering material

The time spent gathering material will depend very much on the demands of the question. You will, however, need to have a clear idea about what you still need to know if you are going to be efficient in finding the right kind of material. Your material is likely to be drawn from a number of different sources – lecture notes, seminar notes, primary texts, secondary or critical texts, and, depending on the question, information from history books, sociology books, dictionaries, encyclopaedias, the internet. Summary skills (see Chapter 5) will be very important here. You may need to be able to sum up the key ideas and arguments of a particular critic, for instance, or summarise some of the different views about, for instance, the role of the poet in the early nineteenth century.

4. Organising and selecting to make a plan

Select and organise your ideas and evidence into a *sequential* argument which uses a *new paragraph for each main idea*. No matter how complicated it is, every building has a ground plan to show how each part relates to the next part. Another way of thinking about it is as a map – you are going to take your reader on a journey and you need to have a route and to be able to rationalise why you have taken this route rather than another. This is where counter-arguments come in – they are very useful as a way of showing what other routes might have been possible and will help to define your particular point of view against alternative points of view.

Your paragraphs are the building blocks of your argument. You need to know how many paragraphs you have, what the function of each paragraph is, what each paragraph needs to make it function properly (sub-points and supporting evidence), and finally how you get from one paragraph to another.

5. Writing your thesis statement

The thesis statement tells the reader what the essay will be about, and what case you, the author, will be making. It's a summary of the argument of the essay and is usually only one sentence, but might be two or three. Sometimes you will choose to incorporate this thesis statement into the introduction, sometimes you will incorporate it into the conclusion, depending on *when* you want the reader to know your argument fully. Wherever you choose to put it, writing it at an early stage will help you stay focused on the question and your answer to it.

6. Writing the main body of the essay

Begin writing according to the plan, altering the plan if necessary as new evidence and ideas arise but always using only evidence that is relevant to your case. Keep the argument close to the surface, summarise one point before you move onto the next point, pay careful attention to transitions from one part of your argument to the next, and make sure that you give each main idea a full paragraph.

7. Writing the introduction

The introduction should be designed to attract the reader's attention and give him or her an idea of the essay's focus. There is no absolute formula for introductions but you are likely to do some or all of the following:

- Focus on the objective of the essay. What is your 'driving' or dominant question? (This is essential.) Tell the reader about it before you begin. Your reader needs an objective too.
- Establish the context of the question you are addressing (this might be historical, sociological, theoretical, scientific, depending upon the question being asked). Set the scene.
- Engage with working definitions of key terms. Are there conflicting definitions? What problems do such definitions throw up? (This will depend upon the terms you are dealing with.)
- Tell the reader why you think the question is important/interesting/relevant?
- Make clear your line of argument and/or indicate the direction you are going to take in answering the question.

8. Writing the conclusion

The conclusion brings closure to the reader, summing up your points or providing a final perspective on your topic. You have been seeking to persuade your reader of your point of view. You have been making a case, so use your final words to make sure you have made it. Be careful not to fizzle out – keep the conclusion strong and authoritative. Refocus the reader's attention on where they started and the point they have reached through your guidance. Some conclusions will summarise the argument, others will look forward to anticipate further questions or issues that arise from the material in the essay. The worst kinds of conclusions are dry, repetitive and/or abrupt.

9. Editing

You have now completed all of the paragraphs of your essay. Before you can consider this a finished product, however, you must give some thought to the formatting of your essay.

- *Check the order of your paragraphs.* Does the argument get lost in places? How can you bring it closer to the surface? Does each paragraph lead on logically from the previous one? Where is the argument strongest/ weakest?
- *Check the instructions for the assignment.* When you prepare a final draft, you must be sure to follow all of the instructions you have been given. Are your margins correct? Have you titled the essay as directed? What other information (name, date, word count, bibliography, references etc.) must you include? Is it properly formatted? Is it well presented?
- *Check your writing.* Nothing can substitute for revision of your work. Redrafting of this kind is most easily done on a word-processor. By review-ing what you have done, you can improve weak points that otherwise would be missed. Read and reread your paper – annotate it with a red pen. Try to anticipate your tutor's comments. Does it make logical sense? Leave it for a few hours and then read it again. Does it still make logical sense? Do the sentences flow smoothly from one another? If not, try to add some words and phrases to help connect them. Transition words and phrases, such as 'therefore' or 'however' or 'on the other hand', sometimes help. Also, you might refer in one sentence to an idea in the previous sen-tence. This is especially useful when you move from one paragraph to another. Have you run a spell checker or a grammar checker? These aids cannot catch every error, but they might catch errors that you have missed. Get your dictionary and check any words you are unsure of.
- *Check your style.* Read your essay aloud to yourself slowly. Is every sentence clear, elegant, fluent, interesting and relevant? Use a thesaurus to extend your vocabulary. Avoid jargon if you can. Unpack sentences that have become too long or convoluted. Is there a single word that will say what you want to say more exactly and economically than that rather

verbose phrase? Alter every word, phrase or sentence that jars on your ear when you read it aloud.

10. Proof-reading

Read your essay one last time. Check that:

- there are no errors of punctuation, spelling, and grammar
- all titles have been properly formatted – inverted commas or italicised
- you have included a properly formatted bibliography
- you have given appropriate references for all the quotes you have used.

When you have checked and corrected all these things write out or print out your final copy.

The process in detail and in practice

We will now look in more detail at the first stages of the essay writing process: the preparation stages. The following chapters will go on to discuss the later stages of writing and editing your work.

1. Thinking about the question

In the interview earlier in this chapter, the lecturer referred to 'knowledge-telling' and 'knowledge-transformation'. These are terms used by two linguists called M. Scardamalia and C. Bereiter who are experts on educational learning processes. They explain that *knowledge-telling* is descriptive and involves recalling and reiterating. It is useful for some kinds of writing such as summaries, surveys, reports, journals and diaries, but it is not appropriate for most kinds of advanced academic writing, which require *knowledge-transformation*. This type of writing involves the transformation of knowledge drawn from a number of different sources used as evidence within a developing argument (Grabe and Kaplan 1996: 5).

So what are the differences in the processes of writing for knowledge-telling and writing for knowledge-transformation? How can you ensure that the writing you produce has transformed the knowledge you have collected into an argument? These two linguists discovered through extensive research that less-skilled writers (those who tend to produce writing of the knowledge-telling kind) generally:

- don't allow time to think through the question and plan out an answer, but begin to write on an assignment almost straight away
- produce much less elaborated sets of pre-writing notes
- usually think about producing content during composing rather than considering problems, issues, goals and plans
- are less likely to undertake major revisions which would involve restructuring the sequence of the argument
- do not tend to make use of main ideas in their writing as guides for planning and integrating information.
  (Scardamalia and Bereiter 1987: 142–75)

In other words, time spent on thinking through the question and the issues it raises, planning out and structuring your ideas and plotting the connections between them is more likely to ensure that you produce an essay based upon knowledge-transformation.

Your tutor will have taken particular care over writing the questions or exam paper. S/he will know the field well, know that there are a number of different issues at stake and probably several competing interpretations or positions on the issue, and be expecting you to take him/her through some of these areas, attempting to assess and resolve some of these issues as you go along, within your own argument. The wording of the question will give you important clues about how you might structure your argument. Broadly, there are seven main types of question you will be asked to answer in higher education: debate, description, evaluation, comparison, exemplification, classification and analysis. Each of these seven types is signalled by particular words.

ACTIVITY 2:

Column 1 contains key words or phrases commonly found in essay questions. Match these to the type of essay in Column 2 which you think you are being asked to produce:

Key words	Type of essay
compare, contrast	debate
classify, describe the types of	description
outline, sketch, summarise	evaluation
illustrate, give examples	comparison
analyse, explain, explore, consider the implications of, in what ways does?	exemplification
assess, justify, to what extent?	classification
discuss, comment (often with a quotation)	analysis

Now identify which of these types of question are going to require most knowledge-telling, and which are going to require the most knowledge-transformation. What types of essay question have you encountered most of all at university?

ACTIVITY 3:

Read through the following questions carefully.

1. 'Lawrence Sterne's narrative methods in general bear a more central relation to the main traditions of the novel than at first appears.' Discuss.
2. 'The most challenging war poems explore the experiences of war rather than protesting against them.' Discuss.
3. In what ways and to what ends do the novels on the course challenge established categories of gender, sexuality and identity?
4. Assess the importance of an understanding of historical/social/cultural context for the analysis and interpretation of *Macbeth*.

Identify the requirements of each essay question, considering the following questions:

- What type of question is this (see table above)?
- What does the essay invite you to do?
- What are the key issues in the question?
- What might be the hidden dangers in the question?
- What are the key terms in the question and what might they mean?
- How might you reformulate the question in your own words in order to show that you understand it?

ACTIVITY 4:

Write a question of your own for each of the seven different types of question for a course on Shakespeare's plays.

2. Brainstorming

In 1858 John Ruskin wrote:

Mostly matters of any consequence are three-sided, or four-sided, or polygonal; and the trotting round a polygon is severe work for people any way stiff in their opinions.

(John Ruskin, from a speech he gave to the Cambridge School of Art in 1858)

Brainstorming is about thinking round the question or 'trotting round the polygon'. The idea is simply to note down as many ideas about your subject and the question topic as you can. It doesn't matter at this stage whether you use full sentences – note form is fine, so long as you will be able to understand it later.

At this stage you need to be able to ask yourself questions – about what you think, about what you know, about where you see connections. If you are not used to doing this you might want to look at the following examples which are typical of the kinds of questions people ask:

- What do you know about ____?
- What do you still need to know?
- What's your position on ____?
- What do others need to know about ____?
- Who is affected by ____?
- How will things change if people change their minds about ____?
- How can people's ideas about ____ be changed?
- When did people first begin to think the way they do about ____?
- Where is support for ____ found?
- Where is opposition to ____ found?
- What are the positions that critics take on this issue?
- Why is it important to convince people about ____?
- What is interesting or important about ____?
- How have things changed since ____?

Some students do this in the form of a spider diagram, with the question or topic in the centre, and many legs coming off the centre circle. This technique is a useful way of mapping out ideas because the way in which they come to us is not in a simple linear structure, but randomly, in different patterns. A spider diagram allows you to group ideas in clusters and to connect up one group of ideas to another by using arrows. It will need to be converted into a linear sequence later, because writing is linear and sequential and you will need to decide what goes in what order and why. But for the moment it is important to produce ideas and to see how one idea might connect to another. You can sort out the order later. Also it's important at this stage to generate as many ideas and questions as you can. You won't be able to use all the material you produce, but deciding what is relevant will be a very important way of focusing on the question in the next stage. See Figure 1 for an example of a spider diagram.

Another method is to outline each of the main ideas on a small piece of paper or card. Then you can set them all out on the floor or on a table and from there you can see how certain ideas might connect with others in a sequence. Once you've put them into some kind of order by arranging them into a pack of cards, you can then check the sequence to see if it works and

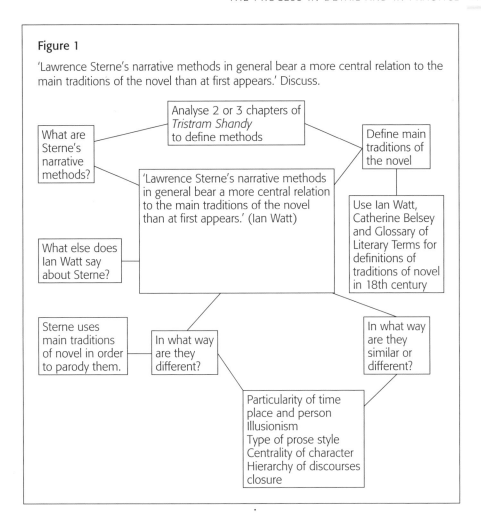

Figure 1

'Lawrence Sterne's narrative methods in general bear a more central relation to the main traditions of the novel than at first appears.' Discuss.

adjust the order again. You can do this with a word-processor, of course, by typing out each of the main ideas briefly and then using the cut and paste options to try out different structures and sequences, but there's something very 'hands-on' and practical about the pieces of card approach.

Another researcher told us of her colour-coding method. Once she had reached the end of the research process and gathered all her material in an exercise book or file, she would go back through the material with high-lighter pens identifying the main ideas in different colours so that she could see the connections quickly. This is also a good method for eliminating non-essential material.

ACTIVITY 5:

Choose a question from a past paper for a course you are currently studying or one of the questions you invented in Activity 4. Produce as many ideas on the question as possible in the form of either a series of notes or a spider diagram.

3. Gathering material

If you've done some careful thinking before you set off for the library, your time spent looking for books and information will be more efficient. You need to know what you are looking for and what questions you have to ask. Knowing what your main questions are and what's relevant is crucial at this stage. You must ask yourself 'what do I still need to know?' The amount you read and the kinds of notes you take depend upon the demands of the particular essay. Remember the following guidelines:

- Be adventurous in how you use the library – if you need historical information find the history section and so on.
- Make full use of computerised information such as the internet, CD-ROM search facilities etc.
- Be open to chance discoveries.
- Use bibliographies from key books and from the course handouts.
- Take notes which sum up the key points of a particular book or critic.
- Always keep a careful record of all your sources and the page numbers of the quotes you want to use.
- Know when to stop: don't use protracted research as an excuse to postpone the painful business of starting to write.

Let's take the essay question above as an example and imagine what a student's thoughts on gathering material might be.

'Lawrence Sterne's narrative methods in general bear a more central relation to the main traditions of the novel than at first appears.' Discuss.

What will my primary texts be? Well, the essay requires me to assess 'Sterne's narrative methods'. The novel I know best is *Tristram Shandy*, because we've studied it in detail on my course. Can I generalise about Sterne's narrative methods from this one novel? I don't think he wrote much else – I'll check this by looking up the entry on Sterne in the *Oxford Companion to English Literature*. Yes, it will be enough for a 3,000-word essay to write only on *Tristram Shandy*, particularly if I justify this decision in my essay.

What will my secondary texts be? The essay asks me to compare Sterne's narrative methods to 'the main traditions of the novel'. I know, because of the course

I'm taking on the eighteenth-century novel, that these refer to the dominance of realism in the Western novel in the late eighteenth and nineteenth centuries. But I also know that I can't talk about realism without spending some time defining what its conventions were (and this is all very complicated). One of the key books about the emergence of realism is Ian Watt, *The Rise of the Novel*. But I also know that this was written some time ago (1957) and that there have been a number of important definitions of realist narrative conventions since then. The one I think I'll use, which is listed in the bibliography, is Catherine Belsey's *Critical Practice* (1980) – there's a section in there which sets out some of the characteristics of the realist tradition. There's also a new book by Lilian Furst called *Realism* (1992) – that might give me a working definition which I could set alongside Watt and Belsey. That's three books on 'the main traditions of the novel'. Too much to read in the time? No, because it will give me the critical range I need and I can read only the relevant passages of each book. It will also help me to define my terms.

I shall also need to look at some books on Sterne himself, particularly books which are interested in his narrative methods. On the course bibliography there's a collection of essays on *Tristram Shandy* edited by Melvyn New, published in 1992. There's bound to be at least one essay on his narrative methods in there. I will also scan along the library shelves to see if there's anything else that will help, particularly critical works on Sterne. If I have time I'll do an MLA search on the computer to see if there are any articles published on Sterne's narrative methods (the Modern Language Association of America database of all journal articles is held on CD-ROM in most university libraries).

What other information sources should I check? I will check the entry on Sterne in *The Oxford Companion to English Literature*. I'll use a *Glossary of Literary Terms* for an entry on realism and traditions of the novel, just to make sure I'm on the right track (the books by Watt, Belsey and Furst will give me all the detail I need). If there's a computer terminal free I'll do an internet search on Sterne as well, which might give me some useful background information.

A final bibliography for this essay, then, might look like this:

Abrams, M.H. (1985) *A Glossary of Literary Terms*, 6th edn. New York: Harcourt Brace Jovanovitch.

Belsey, Catherine (1980) *Critical Practice*. London: Routledge.

Furst, Lilian R. (1992) *Realism*. Harlow: Longman.

New, Melvyn (ed.) (1992) *The Life and Opinions of Tristram Shandy, Gentleman*. New York: St Martin's Press.

Sterne, L. (1967) *The Life and Opinions of Tristram Shandy* [1759–67]. London: Penguin.

Watt, Ian (1957) *The Rise of the Novel: Studies in Defoe, Richardson and Fielding*. London: Peregrine Books.

Annotated bibliography on Sterne on the internet:
http://www.english.upenn.edu/~jlynch/shandy.html

ACTIVITY 6:

Assess the use of material in two or three of your recent academic essays. Check the bibliography against the title and see if you think that you should have drawn on more primary or secondary materials, or chosen materials of a different kind. Define your objective in each of the essays. Did you achieve your objective and in what way did your choice of material help you to achieve this objective?

4. Organising and selecting to make a plan

This is where you will begin to structure the material you have produced into a sequence. Not everyone thinks or argues in straight lines and essay plans can be as complex or straightforward as you make them. A plan doesn't have to travel in absolutely straight lines but it should be clear and easy to work from as you begin to write. Lawrence Sterne himself, in *Tristram Shandy*, complained about the problem of writing in a sequential way:

> Could a historiographer drive on his history, as a muleteer drives on his mule, – straight forward; – for instance, from Rome all the way to Loretto, without ever once turning his head aside either to the right hand or to the left, – he might venture to foretell you to an hour when he should get to his journey's end; – but the thing is, morally speaking, impossible: For, if he is a man of the least spirit he will have fifty deviations from a straight line to make with this or that party as he goes along, which he can no ways avoid. He will have views and prospects to himself perpetually soliciting his eye, which he can no more help standing still to look at than he can fly; he will have various
> Accounts to reconcile;
> Anecdotes to pick up;
> Inscriptions to make out;
> Stories to weave in;
> Tradition to sift;
> . . . In short there is no end of it . . .

(Sterne 1967: 65)

He even drew a diagram of the structure of his book about two-thirds of the way through: see Figure 2. The point, of course, was not only to say 'life's like this, stories are like this', but to send up his own digressive methods in the book too. One of the points he's making in the book is that conventional ways of telling stories in novels make us think that life's neat and ordered and sequential, but, of course, it isn't. However, Sterne's

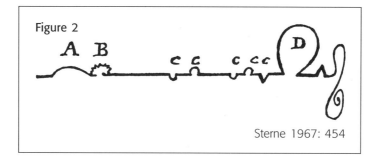

Figure 2

Sterne 1967: 454

narrator, Tristram, never gets to the end of his story, even finds it impossible to begin, because 'there's no end of it' and he never finds a way of selecting out material.

You, however, need to finish your essay in a specific period of time or
you will fail. Your aim is to make an argument, not to show your reader,
like Sterne, that life is complicated and impossible to write about. Con-
sequently, you will need an order and you will need to select your material.
Your reader will read through the essay as a sequence of paragraphs. You
will need to think about the structuring decisions you make in terms of
how successful they will be in persuading your reader of your point of
view. What does my reader need to know first? If I include this part now
will the impact have lessened if I want to return to it later? Shall I put the
counter-arguments first? Should I sum up what I have said so far before I
go on to the next important part of my argument?

This stage of the essay writing process can be very unsettling. There will
be some occasions when your ideas seem so jumbled they simply won't resolve
themselves into a manageable shape. If this does happen it's probably best
to leave it for a short time and return later, or talk it through with a friend,
or go back and read the essay question again. Eventually, when the shape
of the essay does emerge, you will probably wonder why you hadn't
thought of it before because it will seem so obvious.

Although people plan in very different ways there are some general strategies that can be useful:

- Read the essay question again carefully and your own notes about the
  issues it raises.
- Read through all your notes from the brainstorming stage and identify
  the ideas that you think are the most relevant and original.
- Begin to identify the *main* ideas and points.
- Only include material that is absolutely relevant to your argument.
- Don't be tempted to treat the plan as a hold-all in which you stuff every-
  thing you think you might need.
- Come up with some alternative structures for the argument and choose
  the best.

- Make sure that your plan shows the connections between each section and that you understand why you are moving through the material in this particular order.
- Draw up a plan which includes main points, sub-points and the evidence you will use to argue each of these.

In order to give you an example of a brief version of a plan, we will return to the question about Sterne's narrative methods which we began brainstorming above. Drawing up a sketch would be a first stage. The next stage would be to fill in much more detail, indicating which parts of the novel will be used as evidence in sections 3 and 4 of my plan, and short summaries of the Watt, Belsey and Furst arguments for section 2.

'Lawrence Sterne's narrative methods in general bear a more central relation to the main traditions of the novel than at first appears.' Discuss.

I might begin with this as a sketch of a plan:

1. Introduction – the question and its context.
2. Traditions of the novel – Watt, Belsey, Furst used here to define terms and narrative conventions of realist writing.
3. Argument to support the statement: Sterne's narrative methods *do* bear a relation to the traditions of the novel – evidence from text.
4. Argument against the statement: But there are many ways in which Sterne's narrative methods break the rules of the traditional novel – evidence from text.
5. Concluding proposition: Sterne's narrative methods bear a close relation to the main traditions of the novel because one of his concerns is to *parody* the narrative conventions of his time through both mimicry and transgression.

ACTIVITY 7:

Find two or three of your recent essay plans and assess their strengths and weaknesses as plans. Or write an essay plan for an essay question from a course you are currently studying, following the advice you have been given.

5. Writing your thesis statement

What is a thesis statement? 'Thesis' means idea or proposition. It is what you are trying to argue in a particular essay. A thesis statement, then, is like a boiled-down version of your argument. Some people call it an abstract. Ask yourself: what do you want your reader to know or think by the time s/he has finished reading your essay? What position are you arguing? A thesis statement will need to be an answer to the essay question and will probably be inserted either into your introduction or conclusion depending upon *when* you want your reader to have the whole argument summarised for them. You can see a short version of a thesis statement in the concluding section of my plan for the *Tristram Shandy* essay above: 'Sterne's narrative methods bear a close relation to the main traditions of the novel because one of his concerns is to parody the narrative conventions of his time through both mimicry and transgression'.

Why is it important to write your thesis statement before you start writing the essay itself? Won't the main argument just come to you as you write? Yes, for some people it does work like this, but this is often a very lengthy way of arriving at your central idea. It will usually mean that you will have to go back over the essay draft you have already written in order to *refocus* it once you know what your argument is. However, if you have worked this out before you begin you can be more confident that each paragraph you write will be relevant and focused towards arguing this particular case. You will know where you are going and will have a sense of purpose. At each stage in the writing you can refer back to your thesis statement to check that the material you are using is relevant.

Phillis Crème and Mary Lea, in their book *Writing at University*, give the following example which illustrates the close links between thesis statement and structure and shows how important it is to work out the thesis statement (or central idea, as they call it) before you begin:

A biology student was having difficulty in organising her short assignment: 'Discuss the membrane as a link and a barrier'. She had many notes and ideas but she couldn't get them into a shape. As she put it, 'I can't get my plot'. She meant that she could not yet say, 'The central idea of this assignment is . . .'. Without needing to know anything about the subject, you might think an appropriate shape for this piece of writing could be:
1. Introduction: what structural features does the membrane consist of?
2. How the membrane functions as a link.
3. How it functions as a barrier.
4. Conclusion that briefly brings these two aspects together.
But the student couldn't get this to work. As she was talking she suddenly realised that the whole point of what she wanted to say was that the structural features of the membrane worked both as a link and as a barrier at one and the same time. This meant that she had to change her organisation as follows:
1. Introduction: what structural features does the membrane consist of?
2. First structural feature a) as a link and b) as a barrier.
3. Second structural feature a) as a link and b) as a barrier.

4. Conclusion that brings these together: that the same things that make the membrane work as a barrier also make it work as a link.

Now she had her 'plot', her central idea, and could get on with the assignment. She felt that there was a much clearer connection between her introduction and the main part of her assignment, and that it made sense. She was able to construct her story-argument.

(Crème and Lea 1997: 93)

Thesis statements are a statement of the key argument. When you become more practised at writing summaries of your own arguments, you will also improve the summaries you write of other people's arguments. It is very useful to think about finding the key argument when you read any piece of critical writing. For instance, you might conclude: 'In *Shakespeare's Comedies*, Brigitte Smith argues that Shakespeare's comic vision is essentially subversive in that it is directed against tyrannical power systems'.

ACTIVITY 8:

Read the following two abstracts of papers given at a recent academic conference on the relationship between Romanticism and Victorianism. Abstracts are written to give people a brief idea of what the conference paper (twenty minutes long) will be arguing, so they are in essence longer versions of thesis statements, longer because they need to tell the audience something about what will be *in* the paper as well as what it is arguing. They are usually assembled into a short booklet which the delegates use to decide which sessions they will go to, so one of the objectives of the writers is not just to sum up the argument but also to make it sound interesting enough to draw an audience.

Identify the key sentence or sentences in each of the abstracts – the part that states the argument or the thesis statement. Where does this fall in the piece itself – beginning, middle or end? How clear is it? In your own words sum up the argument of each piece in one sentence.

'Elegiac Voices: Wordsworth, Turner and Ruskin' by Dinah Birch, University of Oxford.

When Ruskin published the first volume of *Modern Painters* in 1843, he was an ambitious young man, twenty-four years old, announcing himself as the champion of the modern rather than the ancient in culture. Yet there is a persistently retrospective cast to his critical thought. The epigraph to his pioneering book, and to each of the four subsequent volumes of this monumental early Victorian work (1843–60), is taken from Wordsworth's *The Excursion* (1814), and its great hero among painters is Turner. Both Wordsworth (1770–1850) and Turner (1775–1851) are revolutionary Romantic figures whose continuing presence in Victorian culture Ruskin interprets for his own generation. In doing so, he makes significant changes in perceptions of their cultural role. Looking at their work through the medium of his own remembered childhood, he identifies memory and elegy as the central impulses of their thought, and refigures the energy of their Romantic visions of nature into something darker and potentially more destructive. In the development of the complex and far-reaching theories of *Modern Painters*, it is possible to trace some of the most influential critical interfaces between radical Romanticism and its sober legacies in early Victorian culture.

(By kind permission of the author)

'Byron and Clough: Tourists and Lovers' by Drummond Bone, University of Glasgow.

I will be looking at rhymes and cadences in *Beppo* and *Amours de Voyages* as a way of talking about freedom and contingency, convention and commitment in the sceptical Romantic tradition. I will argue that Clough's hexameters have a family relationship with Byron's ottava rima stanza, and that both poets' concern with the systole-diastole of tolerance and loss-of-value is wrapped up with their formal self-reflexivity.

(By kind permission of the author)

ACTIVITY 9:

Choose an essay in a critical book listed in a bibliography for one of the courses or modules you are currently studying. Read the essay through as carefully as you need to in order to be able to write a thesis statement for that essay. Write up the thesis statement in the form of a short conference abstract. Remember that you will need to make it sound inviting as well as outlining its argument.

ACTIVITY 10:

Make some notes on your current skills as a writer of academic essays, considering the stages of the essay writing process we have discussed so far: thinking about the question, brainstorming, gathering material, planning, and defining your thesis statement. What are your strengths and weaknesses? Do you write essays as a sequenced argument? Do you follow the stages of essay writing outlined above? Which stages do you skimp on? Which stages do you do best/badly/not at all? What have your teachers and tutors said about your strengths and weaknesses as a writer of academic essays? What skills do you need to work on to improve your marks?

If you are working in groups, each person should summarise their notes to the rest of the group. Discuss any points that have come up from this exercise. Are there common patterns, weaknesses, strengths you share as a group? Produce a very brief list of points.

Summary

In this chapter we have examined:

- the process of essay writing
- the first five stages of that process:
  - thinking about the question
  - brainstorming
  - gathering material
  - planning
  - writing a thesis statement.

References

Abrams, M.H. (1985) *A Glossary of Literary Terms*, 6th edn. New York: Harcourt Brace Jovanovitch.

Belsey, Catherine (1980) *Critical Practice*. London: Routledge.

Crème, Phillis and Lea, Mary R. (1997) *Writing at University: A Guide for Students*. Buckingham: Open University Press.

Furst, Lilian R. (1992) *Realism*. Harlow: Longman.

Grabe, William and Kaplan, Robert (1996) *Theory and Practice of Writing*. Harlow: Longman.

New, Melvyn (ed.) (1992) *The Life and Opinions of Tristram Shandy, Gentleman*. New York: St Martin's Press.

Scardamalia, M. and Bereiter, C. (1987) 'Knowledge Telling and Knowledge Transformation in Written Composition' in S. Rosenberg (ed.), *Advances in Applied Psycholinguistics. Vol. 2: Reading, Writing and Language Learning*. Cambridge and New York: Cambridge University Press.

Sterne, L. (1967) *The Life and Opinions of Tristram Shandy* [1759–67]. London: Penguin.

Watt, Ian (1957) *The Rise of the Novel: Studies in Defoe, Richardson and Fielding*. London: Peregrine Books.

Annotated bibliography on Sterne on the internet: http://www.english.upenn.edu/~jlynch/shandy.html

CHAPTER

Paragraphs: the building blocks of essays

Peter Chapman

C hapter 3 gave you an overview of the essay writing process divided into ten stages and we took you through stages 1 to 5, from thinking about the question to writing a thesis statement. We also discussed the special character of academic writing: its focus on the relationship between argument and evidence in relation to a particular topic. In this chapter, we shall continue to think about argument and evidence by exploring actual examples of academic essays so that we can guide you in how to handle stages 6 to 8 of the process. This chapter, therefore, will concentrate on:

- stage 6: writing the main body of the essay
- stage 7: writing the beginning of the essay
- stage 8: writing the ending of the essay.

In thinking about stages 6 to 8, we will:

- focus on the composition of paragraphs as the building blocks of essay writing
- analyse an essay on Jane Austen published in 1990 by a leading academic critic of English literature, David Lodge, as an example of successful practice
- ask you to examine a selection of student essays – so it would be useful to collect two or three examples of your own recent essays or those of other students before you begin.

At this point you need to read David Lodge's essay, which is to be found at the end of this book. You may wish to read it several times, as one quick read will not ensure sufficient familiarity for the following discussion.

Remember, when you are reading, that David Lodge is a critic with years of experience of interpreting texts and writing academic essays. Don't be intimidated or feel that your essays have to copy his work slavishly. But his essay does provide you with a model of how to structure an argument. It will also give you practice in reading literary criticism, which you will need to do when gathering material for your own essays.

The paragraph as the building block of essays

Essays are made from groups of statements placed in a logical order. These are grouped in paragraphs to form coherent, relatively self-contained units. A sequence of these units makes up an essay – but it also composes an argument which responds to a question or develops a topic. Before we start thinking about how ideas are organised into an argument in an essay, we need to look at the composition of paragraphs.

How many elements are there in a paragraph? How flexible or rigid should a paragraph be? Should the one-sentence paragraph, regularly used in tabloid newspapers, be avoided, and if so why? Remember, we are dealing with paragraphs and paragraphing in *academic* writing, a particular variety or kind of writing: some of the things we say may not be applicable to other varieties of writing, like tabloid newspapers, personal letters, or advertisements.

There are several important things to remember when constructing paragraphs in academic essays. There is a distinction between the *parts* and the *paragraphs* of an essay. By parts we mean the main divisions of the structure of an essay: the beginning, the main body, the ending. The main body of the essay will be divided into a number of paragraphs. The beginning and ending of the essay may well be more than one paragraph each as well. Each point in the essay may be discussed in one paragraph, or may need two, or even three, linked paragraphs to discuss it fully. So, essays are built up of interlocking paragraphs which relate ideas, or parts of ideas, together in a logical sequence.

Paragraphs are not all the same length in academic essays: the length of a paragraph is determined by how much there is to say about a particular point. Paragraphs which are very short, or very long, should, on the whole, be avoided: if you find yourself writing these then there may be something wrong with your arrangement of points, i.e. with your essay plan. Also remember that paragraphs need to be related to each other using linking devices and that you need to sustain a logical progression of thought within paragraphs.

Paragraph structure in David Lodge's essay on Jane Austen

To explore these points in more detail we are going to pick out two or three paragraphs from David Lodge's essay and explore his technique. The essay contains twenty-two paragraphs: a one-paragraph introduction; a main body which consists of twenty-one paragraphs and discusses about fifteen separate points; and a conclusion which, though it does not have a separate paragraph to itself, is unmistakably the conclusion, as you will see when we come to it. Now read paragraphs 1 to 8 of Lodge's essay.

Welcome back. We are now going to focus, first of all, on paragraph 5:

The classic love story consists of a delay not only of the heroine's desire but also of the reader's desire – to know the answer to the basic question raised by the narrative: will the heroine get the man she wants? There are three principal sources of interest in narrative: suspense, mystery and irony. Suspense raises the question: what will happen? Mystery raises the question: why did it happen? When the reader knows the answer to the question but the characters do not, irony is generated. Thus, all rereadings of novels tend to create irony, but this is especially true of Jane Austen's novels, which are permeated with irony, rhetorical as well as dramatic, and which can sustain an infinite number of readings. On first reading they tend, like most love stories, to engage the reader's interest through suspense rather than mystery. *Emma* is an exception, since it is full of enigmas (Why is Mr Elton so keen to attend the Westons' dinner party when Harriet is ill? Who sent the piano to Jane Fairfax? What are Frank Churchill's real feelings about Emma?). This follows from the fact that Emma does not fall in love until the book is almost over; therefore, the question: will she get the man she wants? cannot provide the main source of narrative interest. In *Pride and Prejudice* too, though to a lesser extent, the heroine's knowledge of her own heart is delayed, and enigmas, mainly to do with Wickham and Darcy, supply narrative interest, together with the suspense plot concerning Bingham's intention toward Elizabeth's sister Jane. In the other novels Jane Austen makes relatively little use of mystery as a means of engaging the reader's interest, and in *Northanger Abbey* she mocked Mrs Radcliffe's rather mechanical reliance on this device in *The Mysteries of Udolpho* (1794).

What are we looking for when we consider the structure of this paragraph? To summarise, we are looking for:

- a topic sentence
- extension of the topic statement

- evidence to support the topic sentence
- further comment on that evidence
- a concluding sentence which prepares the reader for the next paragraph.

ACTIVITY 1:

Identify the following elements in the above paragraph:

- Is there *one main idea* in the paragraph? Summarise it in your own words. Does Lodge digress from this main point? List his digressions.
- The sentence which states the main idea of the paragraph is called the *topic sentence*. This sentence is usually at or near the beginning of the paragraph, although it could also be the concluding sentence of the paragraph. Where is this sentence in Lodge's paragraph?
- Often, however, one sentence is not enough to elucidate fully the main idea of the paragraph, so there will be further comment on or *extension of the topic sentence*. Can you find this in Lodge's paragraph?
- It is very important to be clear that a topic sentence and its extension do not simply reproduce details from the text: you need to do more with a topic sentence than show that you have read the book. The topic sentence and its extension contribute to the *argument*, so they will make a claim or offer a particular interpretation of aspects of the text. Do you remember the distinction between knowledge-telling and knowledge-transformation? We are looking for the latter here. What is Lodge's argument: how does he transform rather than merely describe the information?
- Next come the details, or *evidence*, which will support your topic sentence and its extension. Evidence can take the form of specific details from the text to do with characterisation, setting, events, and the literary techniques used to convey these aspects of the text. It can also take the form of quotations from the text, or from relevant critical works. What evidence does Lodge use to support his topic sentence?
- Remember that *examples or quotations* may need further comment or interpretation. Make sure you are not just stringing quotations together. If you include them, you need to show which points they are supporting and why they are relevant: you need to interpret them. Look at paragraphs 6 and 7 in Lodge's essay. How does he use quotation? Is it effective?
- Finally, the paragraph needs to *conclude*. This may be through a summary sentence, or a sentence which prepares the reader for the next paragraph. How does Lodge close paragraph 5?

Let's think about the answers to the questions in Activity 1. Does Lodge's fifth paragraph include all these points? Surely it does. The topic sentence makes a claim about the narrative essence of 'the classic love story': it names this as 'delay'. You could argue that the real topic sentence is actually the second sentence with its very knowledgeable definition of narrative, but this second sentence is perhaps best seen as extension of the first sentence because it says what the effects of 'delay' are: 'suspense', 'mystery' and 'irony'. Lodge then comments in general terms on Jane Austen's special emphasis on irony before making a smooth transition to some examples of these narrative structures or strategies from the three novels. The paragraph ends with reference to a fourth novel by Jane Austen, *Northanger Abbey*, which then becomes the focus of the next paragraph, and a new topic sentence which claims that Jane Austen 'played a delightful (and risky) double game with . . . conventions' in this novel. So there is a preparation made for the next paragraph, thus completing all the elements of the academic paragraph we set out above.

ACTIVITY 2:

Read paragraphs 6 and 7 of the essay. Analyse both paragraphs looking for the elements we have demonstrated above. Find the topic sentence, or sentences, write it/them down, and then write brief notes on the other elements. Analyse, in particular, how the transition from paragraph 6 to paragraph 7 is made. Do you think these two paragraphs might have been better as one paragraph, or do you think two are preferable? Why?

Lodge's essay structure: the larger picture

We have analysed the structure of individual paragraphs. Now we need to think about how these paragraphs fit into the essay as a whole. Let's think about paragraph 5 first. What is the relevance of this paragraph on 'the classic love story' and 'the sources of interest in narrative' to Lodge's title and overall argument? How does it earn its keep? The short answer is that 'the classic love story' is incorporated into the eighteenth-century 'sentimental novel' which Lodge describes at the beginning of the essay. But we can say more than that. Earlier on, we said that Lodge's essay consists of twenty-one paragraphs and discusses about fifteen separate points. We now need to say more about these 'separate points.' These need to be understood as feeding into, or establishing, the three main concerns of the essay as a whole. These three main concerns are introduced at the very beginning of the essay. They are: 'the sentimental novel', 'the comedy of manners', and 'the (unprecedented) effect of realism' introduced in Jane Austen's novels.

So we can now say that the essay consists of three main concerns, about fifteen points, and twenty-one paragraphs, and that there isn't a one-to-one relationship between points and paragraphs because some points need to be developed over more than one paragraph.

ACTIVITY 3:

In order to grasp fully the structure of Lodge's essay, write an essay plan for it. Decide what the main points are which contribute to the three main concerns (as above). Find the main topic sentences which introduce these main points, and write these down. Do not include in your search the first paragraph or the last eight lines of the last paragraph. Remember that you will not be writing down the topic sentence for every paragraph, but only those which state the main points. This will mean you will need to note which paragraphs contain the main topic sentences and which paragraphs have the job of continuing the discussion of the main points.

Linking paragraphs

All writers of argument-and-evidence essays (academic essays) need to show the links between the sequence of paragraphs which make up the structure of points in an essay. 'However' and 'therefore', as first words in paragraphs, are tried and tested, familiar linking devices implying development and sequence. But it is important to move beyond relying on just a few, often repeated words and phrases. Here are some of the ways David Lodge links the paragraphs in his Austen essay:

Linking devices with key words or phrases in italics	Comment
Paragraph 2 begins: 'By the "sentimental novel", *in this context*, I mean ...'	'in this context' refers back to a central idea in the previous paragraph
Paragraph 3 begins: 'Structurally, *then*, ...'	'then' means 'drawing out the implications of the previous paragraph'
Paragraph 7 begins: '*But* as several commentators have observed ...'	'but' means 'there is a point to make which is contrary to the one in the previous paragraph'
Paragraph 12 begins: '*For example*, Roland Barthes's analysis ...'	here a key example for a point which has already been made is given a separate paragraph of its own
Paragraph 22 begins: '*Emma* follows an *antithetical* method.'	i.e. 'I am going to discuss an example which implies the opposite of my previous example'
Paragraph 19 ends: 'This brings us to the topic of "point of view".'	this takes the reader straight on to the next paragraph

---

ACTIVITY 4:

Look for three more ways of linking paragraphs and sequences of ideas in Lodge's essay. Then select one of the essays you collected at the beginning of the chapter (it might be one of your own or an essay written by another student). Write notes on the linking methods used in this essay. Consider any strengths and weaknesses you perceive in the writer's methods of linking paragraphs.

The art of introduction

We cannot exaggerate the importance of an essay's introduction. The fact that we are dealing with this crucial part of an essay in second place in this chapter does not mean that it is of secondary significance. But we wanted to deal very thoroughly with how most paragraphs in essays are handled – in the main body of the essay – before turning to those 'star' paragraphs, the beginning and the ending.

Introductory paragraphs do not work quite like those in the main body because they have different functions to perform. Let us look at Lodge's introduction and also at the title of his essay:

'Composition, distribution, arrangement: form and structure in Jane Austen's novels'

Each of Jane Austen's novels has its own distinctive identity, but they also have a strong family resemblance, one to another. What kind of fiction did she write, and what was special about it? The short answer is that she fused together the sentimental novel and the comedy of manners with an unprecedented effect of realism. A longer answer will entail a description of these categories and qualities in terms of narrative form and structure.

At first sight, Lodge's title seems rather uninspiring – it appears narrowly technical and a bit 'lifeless'. But Lodge is not a 'lifeless' writer and we shall discover that he has a trick up his sleeve when we get to the conclusion of his essay. Let us, for the moment, say that the title is *apparently* rather flat, but also point out that it is an accurate title: the essay does have a lot to say about the forms or conventions of fiction that Jane Austen inherited – and which she calmly proceeded to transform.

The introduction contains four sentences. Please read them through again. Let us consider the function of each:

1. Each of Jane Austen's novels has its own distinctive identity, but they also have a strong family resemblance, one to another.

This sentence does not seem to be doing absolutely vital work: what it says is surely true of any serious novelist, so strictly speaking it states the obvious. Its function seems to be to use a short sentence to get the ball rolling, and in fact we would advise against such an opening in your own essays because the temptation to state the obvious is best resisted. It can often be a way of avoiding deciding on and putting your argument into words, a challenging but vital activity. We will let Lodge off if he can produce an impressive second sentence.

> 2. What kind of fiction did she write, and what was special about it?

Well, yes! This sentence tells us that Lodge is going to take on major questions about Jane Austen's art, her place in the history of English fiction, and the reasons why she has always been appreciated and enjoyed. So this is Lodge's 'driving question' (see Chapter 3). On literature courses, the driving question is often in the essay title that has been set. In this case, the question might be: 'Why are Jane Austen's novels distinctive?'

> 3. The short answer is that she fused together the sentimental novel and the comedy of manners with an unprecedented effect of realism.

This is the crucial sentence. Note that it contains the three themes which form the three major concerns of the essay, and note that it is the *thesis statement* for the whole essay: its central argument. It is not simply an obviously true statement such as 'All Jane Austen's novels end in marriage'. It is an argumentative contention, a claim which might be plausible or might not be. It is one the writer is going to have to find evidence for in the details and qualities of the novels, and in what other critics have argued. Lodge's claim is that Jane Austen took two existing literary forms or genres – the eighteenth-century sentimental novel and the age-old comedy of manners (which in her day was a theatrical genre) – and from these, she produced a new kind of novel which was more realistic than other eighteenth- and early nineteenth-century novels. So sentence 3 sets up the essay by stating its argument, briefly, right at the beginning.

> 4. A longer answer will entail a description of these categories and qualities in terms of narrative form and structure.

Lodge does not define his terms in his introduction. This is because he is going to devote one half of his essay to defining and illustrating the ideas of the 'sentimental novel' and 'comedy of manners' as handled by Jane Austen and other novelists of the period, and one half to how Jane Austen achieves an 'effect of realism' that these other writers could not manage. Sentence 4, then, has the function of indicating to the reader what to expect in the essay as a whole. This is always worth doing. As it says in Chapter 3: '[write a] statement of your argument and/or an indication of the direction you are going to take in your answer'. Lodge does *both*, in, respectively, sentence 3 and sentence 4.

You will have noticed that Lodge's introduction is very short – shorter in fact than is usual for either published or student essays. We are not recommending that your introductions are as compressed as this (one reason why Lodge's is so compressed is that he is saving his surprise until the end, as you will see). What we *do* wish to emphasise is that you should consider function before length, and make the function determine the length.

If Lodge had wanted to be more explicit (though it would have spoiled his surprise) he could have written:

> Earlier generations of readers of Jane Austen often wrote about her work as though it were charmingly entertaining and delightfully free from complications or technical difficulties. Such a view, however, completely disregards, or even fails to notice, the extraordinary skill with which her novels are composed and the major contribution she made to solving some of the technical obstacles to artistic maturity in the narrative forms she inherited from the eighteenth century.

An opening like this would signal that the essay is going to be focused on both historical and stylistic issues and could then lead straight to sentence 2. This would produce a longer introduction, but not necessarily a better one (see the section below on 'The Art of Concluding' for further comment).

ACTIVITY 5:

Here are the title and introduction to a student essay on Jane Austen and other women writers. Using our guidelines on composing introductions, write notes on the strengths and/or weaknesses of this introduction. What is the argument, or thesis statement? How might you improve it? You might rearrange, take out, or add elements in relation to the title.

> **'The portrayal of emotion in a domestic, family setting': does this kind of expectation of female fiction writing represent a constraint or an opportunity for women writers of the period 1780–1860?**
>
> The question of whether the woman writer of the period 1780–1860 was able to write about the same subjects as men and if so, what relevance it had to literature as a whole is a question which is only now being raised by twentieth-century scholars.
>
> The expectations others had of the middle-class woman of this period (women writers of this period were mostly middle-class) were extremely limited. This is obvious when we study the conduct books of the time.

> My argument will be to prove that 'the portrayal of emotions in a domestic, family setting' represents an opportunity for women writers as it provides them with the liberty to tackle issues within and beyond their immediate experience.

ACTIVITY 6:

Select one of the essays you collected at the beginning of this chapter. Read it through thoroughly, examining each of the paragraphs carefully. Identify the topic sentences in each paragraph. Does each paragraph have such a sentence? If there doesn't seem to be one in a particular paragraph, try to write a topic sentence for it. Do the topic sentences make up a sequence of points which can be related back to the title and introduction? Do these points form a logical order? Do you think there is a need for further points and/or do you think any of the points are not needed in the essay as a whole? Write up a short analysis.

ACTIVITY 7:

Here are two more titles and introductions to student essays. One is on First World War poetry and the other is on Bram Stoker's *Dracula*. How successful are they? Bearing in mind the advice you have been given in this chapter about writing introductions, write a short assessment of their strengths and weaknesses as introductions.

> **'The most challenging war poems explore the experiences of war rather than protesting against them.' Discuss.**
>
> When a poem sets out to explore and experience war, a special construction is often called for, disturbing images and unsettling diction being widely used throughout the most convincing poems, to explore and depict the surrounding carnage and hostility. Often the politics and protests of the poet are made more apparent by the absence of comment in the poems. The effect of this use of understated protest leads the reader to form their own outrage at the constant ordeals and the altered mentality of the soldiers that have to endure all the horrors of war. In this way poetry that examines war and its horrors is thought to be revolutionary. I have chosen two exemplary examples of poems which although they examine war, they do not openly protest against war. The poems are: 'The Silent One' by Ivor Gurney, and 'Strange Meeting' by Wilfred Owen.

> **Bram Stoker's *Dracula*: a metamorphosing masterpiece.**
>
> *Dracula* has received more attention than any of Bram Stoker's other numerous works. It is not, however, only Stoker's other works that the novel has overshadowed, but also all previous vampire myths, as it has become the most popular and renowned

vampire story in the twentieth century. Since it was first published, nearly a hundred years ago, in 1897, the novel has never gone out of print. It has been translated into many different languages, been adapted into hundreds of different film versions, television programmes, inspired cartoon characters, as well as becoming a household name. Why has the impact of this story been so great in popular culture that its presence has been constant enough to make the figure of Count Dracula one of the dominant icons of the twentieth century? Its popularity seems to suggest some sort of deeply felt relevance or significance among generation after generation of audiences.

ACTIVITY 8:

Take three essay questions which you have been given and, in one sentence, write an opening argumentative statement which you could use to answer them. Make sure you are not just *describing* the topic, but *arguing* for a particular interpretation or slant on the question.

In summary, then, introductions to essays need to do four things:

- catch the reader's attention
- introduce the argument of the essay through a thesis statement in direct response to the question
- introduce the main concerns of the essay
- provide some context for your argument.

The art of concluding

How does Lodge conclude his essay? He provides an excellent solution to the advice in Chapter 3 to make sure that you do not fizzle out at the end; keep the conclusion strong and authoritative; refocus the reader's attention on where they started and the point they have reached; and avoid the worst kind of conclusion which is dry, repetitive and/or abrupt.

The two main approaches to conclusions are:

- to link up with the introduction and/or the title and draw together all the points you have been making in a broad statement
- to anticipate further questions and issues that arise from the material in the essay, i.e. put the themes you have discussed into a wider context.

In a sense, Lodge does both, although it might be argued that he is really using the first approach. Here is Lodge's conclusion, which is tucked quietly away at the end. It could have been presented as a separate paragraph, but the rhetorical effect would have been somewhat lost, as you will see.

> . . . To make that comparison [i.e. between Jane Austen's skills and Henry James's] inevitably recalls the astonishing perversity of James's own observation that 'Jane Austen was *instinctive and charming*. . . . For signal examples of what *composition, distribution, arrangement* can do, of how they intensify the life of the work of art, we have to go elsewhere.' He never said an untruer word. (our italics)

At last, as we link together Lodge's title, his introduction and his conclusion, we are able to appreciate his 'little surprise'. What looked like a lifeless part of the title ('composition, distribution, arrangement') is suddenly revealed to be a phrase used by Henry James in his downgrading of Jane Austen's skills as an artist and novelist. A brief note on Henry James's standing in English literature might be useful at this point. Writing at the turn of the twentieth century, he was not only a highly respected novelist but also one of the first writers in English to produce theory and criticism of the novel as an art form. What Henry James said about Jane Austen is, then, of some importance – especially if he is wrong, as Lodge, we now realise, has set out to demonstrate. Note the emotional expression – 'astonishing perversity' – that Lodge uses to express his disagreement with James: this is clearly an issue Lodge cares about. But note also the fair-mindedness that goes with the commitment: James may have misjudged Jane Austen, but his powers as a novelist were equal to hers. Lodge's punch-line, his final flourish, is itself verbally skilful: he takes a popular expression and gives it a twist: 'he never said an *untruer* word' (italics ours).

Lodge ends his essay with a clever word play which itself is like one of the delicate but hard-hitting ironies in Jane Austen's own style. Essays don't, obviously, have to end in this clever way, but in general you should make sure that your conclusions do two things: refer back to your argument or thesis statement, and provide closure by summarising where your discussion has taken you or by pointing to further questions or topics for debate in relation to the thesis statement. You should avoid merely reiterating your thesis statement. The essay is like a journey; it should have taken you somewhere that is different from where you started. This could mean that you have a new angle on the thesis statement which you offer at the end, or that by accruing evidence and examples you have come to a fuller, more detailed version of the thesis statement.

ACTIVITY 9:

Here is the conclusion to the student's essay on Jane Austen and other women writers, referred to in Activity 5 above:

I agree with Virginia Woolf that women writers of the earlier nineteenth century showed great integrity to continue producing such great work under constant and painful criticism. Middle-class women of this period were constrained by society in what they thought, learnt and did. It is due to this condition that the women writers of this period tended towards the domestic, family setting. This, however, was by no means a constraint on the portrayal of emotions in my opinion. On the contrary, as Woolf said, 'the novel has this correspondence to real life, its values are to some extent those of real life'. The women writers studied in this course were writing about real life as they knew it to be.

Consider this conclusion in relation to the title and the introduction to the essay you read earlier. Write notes on the strengths and any weaknesses of the conclusion. What changes could be made to improve it?

ACTIVITY 10:

Select one of the student essays you gathered at the beginning of this chapter. Read this essay through carefully before attempting the following activities.

- Analyse and assess the quality of the introduction to the essay. In particular, is the argument clearly stated in this introduction? If not, where is it stated?
- How many separate points does the essay discuss in its main body? Is it possible to identify the topic sentences for these points? How many paragraphs are there for each point?
- What different kinds of evidence does the essay employ to support its points and its overall argument?
- Analyse and assess the quality of the essay's conclusion.

Argument, evidence and coherence in two very good paragraphs

You will by now have realised that when paragraphs are not entirely successful it is usually because they lack, within themselves, one or more of the following: an orderly sequence, a logical progression from point to point, a balance between the claims made and the evidence offered, and a lack of integration with what comes before or after. They often also lack lucid statements of the points you wish to make so that the expression clutters up the argument. Clarity of expression, of course, goes hand-in-hand with clarity of mind and organisation. If you know what you want to say, you can say it clearly (though sometimes after several attempts).

Here are two paragraphs from a recent, well-regarded history book. You don't need to know anything at all about the subject they discuss to appreciate them. We are interested in them because the argument they contain is clearly developed, balanced, judicious and lucid. In other words they embody many of the virtues looked for in all academic writing. But what exactly is so good about them? Read them through and make some notes on what impresses you about them, especially about the stages through which the argument goes. Can you summarise it succinctly? (The issues under consideration are the causes and effects of the growth in population during Britain's industrial revolution.)

The main issue of the debate centres on the validity of the contention by G.T. Griffiths in 1926, and confirmed with reservations by T.H. Marshall, that the major cause of the population growth was the decline in the death rate, arising from the advance of medical science, perhaps the most signific- ant contribution being the discovery by Jenner of vaccination as a precau- tion against the notorious killer, smallpox. The effect of this, however, would have made little impact until the early years of the nineteenth century. In recent years emphasis has tended to switch to the rising of the birth rate, partly as a result of women marrying younger (according to analysis in 1981 by E.A. Wrigley and R.S. Schofield into what economists describe as 'nuptuality' statistics).[10]

An increasing demand for labour at a time when industry was expanding might also have encouraged larger families. But the rapidity with which the booms were followed by slumps during the nineteenth century presents such a picture of fluctuating fortunes that this last argument seems difficult to sustain. Furthermore, different environments created different situations. This has been borne out by recent research into the lowering of the age at which women married. Just a single instance will suffice, for the year 1861. In Sheffield – the centre of the steel and cutlery industry – 85 per cent of the female population were married by the age of 30; whereas in Keighley, a wool textile town, the percentage was only 69. It is a reasonable deduction that women living in centres of heavy industry, where there was little opportunity for employment, would marry at an earlier age than their coun- terparts in textile towns where they could more easily obtain paid work.[11]

Notes

10. M.J. Daunton, *Progress and Poverty: An Economic and Social History of Britain 1700–1850* (Oxford, 1995), pp. 392–6.
11. *Ibid.*, 401; the statistics are taken from R.I. Woods and P.R.A. Hinde, 'Nuptuality and Age of Marriage in Nineteenth-Century England', *Journal of Family History*, 10 (1985), 125.

(Newsome 1998: 16–17)

What is admirable here?

There is the clarity of the organisation and expression. As we said above, clarity of expression goes hand in hand with clarity of thought and organisation. If you know what you want to say, you have more chance of saying it clearly. Here, the points move from one to another with impeccable lucidity. The sentences are well-judged in length and structure. They are straightforward and carry just the right amount of information to be held in the mind at one point in a quite complex sequence of points overall. On the other hand they are not monotonously short, or robotically repetitive in structure, making them as dull to read as a statistical table. This is an *argument*, remember, in which a human being (you, the writer) is speaking to another (the reader).

The argument develops logically from point to point. The reader isn't left wondering what will come next or how have we got from there to here. There's a logical, coherent arrangement of the points under discussion which sustains an unfolding consideration of the topic. In a sense, this argument (as you have it here) lacks a classic 'topic sentence'. That, actually, comes on the previous page a paragraph or two earlier. It reads as follows: 'But what answer could the Victorians give to the most perplexing question of all? They knew that the population had increased and was continuing to increase; but they did not know why' (Newsome 1998: 15). What you have in these two paragraphs are a mixture of an extension of a topic sentence and an account of the evidence. It is a survey of the ideas of modern historians on this topic which comes to no firm conclusion. Afterwards, Newsome considers some Victorian responses. This procedure is quite common in academic argument for the obvious reason that there are many questions to which there are no decisive answers, though there are frequently strong views of various kinds. Newsome's appraisal appears to be a carefully arranged presentation of the various options.

There is a judicious weighing up of the evidence which is given to the reader with great skill. Each position on the population issue is sketched succinctly with just enough detail to give it substance, but not so much that it will distract from the main line of thought. Look how skilfully the detail of Jenner's discovery is deployed. Look at how effective the simple phrase 'Just a single instance will suffice' can be. The accumulation of *just enough* detail gains our confidence. Here's someone who knows the material; here's someone who knows where they are going (even if the conclusion is that nobody really knows); here's somebody I'm happy to follow to the next point. A reader will pay more attention to what you have to say if you have gained his or her trust in this way by a thoughtful choice of what information to deliver.

The passage maintains admirable focus throughout. There are no distractions or digressions, no red herrings, no points where we scratch our heads and say 'eh?'

Though the passage comes to no firm, overall conclusion, it does not leave you in the same place at the end as you were at the beginning. You do not feel 'well, I know no more now than I did to start off with'. You know that this is a very complicated issue; you know that a good deal of detailed, scholarly work has been done; you know what some of that is; you know that some explanations work in Keighley but not in Sheffield; and you will shortly know (if you read the book) that the Victorians had some daft and not-so-daft ideas about the same puzzling, crucially important phenomenon. In short, the passage not only demonstrates how to develop an argument. It informs you about the details of a debate, and embodies a crucial truth about intelligent discussion: sometimes it's impossible to know the answer, but it's always best to know what you are talking about.

Why are there two paragraphs here? Would one have done? After all, both follow the same topic. In fact, the division into two paragraphs (which are pretty equally balanced in terms of length) is to help the reader. The paragraph break doesn't mark a change in direction in the argument or move to a new topic. It's a pause for breath, a chance for the reader to reflect on the progress of the argument, to assimilate the complex array of information. Note how each begins with a clear statement of the issue under consideration, and how each ends in a rounded way, skilfully and clearly signalling the close of the point it is making.

Note the referencing. This is a richly informed piece of writing, based on a lot of reading, but it carries this learning lightly. There are two references and each manages very concisely to give the reader an authority for the claims being made, a source for the information, and something further to read should they wish to do so. The passage isn't choked with notes and references like academic hiccups so you can't follow the argument for the references. But nor is it just brazenly assertive, as naked as the emperor in his new clothes. It is part of intelligent academic discussion, when you read something, to check up and find out more. It is part of effective academic writing to help your reader do this.

Many of these points are of crucial importance for the way you structure arguments over a longer duration than two paragraphs. For this (as well as effective paragraph writing) you need to appreciate how to maintain an argument ensuring logical sequence and overall coherence.

Summary

In this chapter we have covered the following points:

- the importance of argument in an essay: knowledge-transformation rather than knowledge-telling
- the relationship between parts (beginning, main body and ending) and paragraphs in an essay
- the relationship between points and paragraphs in an essay

- the relationship between points in an essay as the main arguments are developed
- structure within paragraphs
- topic sentences
- extension of topic sentences
- linking paragraphs together
- beginnings
- endings.

References

Lodge, David (1990) 'Composition, Distribution, Arrangement: Form and Structure in Jane Austen's Novels' in *After Bakhtin: Essays on Fiction and Criticism*. London: Routledge.

Newsome, David (1998) *The Victorian World Picture: Perceptions and Introspections in an Age of Change*. London: Fontana.

Summary skills

Nora Crook

Every day, we explain, simplify and shorten our thoughts and our speech. We do not recall, say or write all that we are theoretically capable of recalling, saying or writing – which is just as well, as verbal traffic would otherwise be gridlocked. The same is true of the printed word. We are constantly clarifying and condensing information both to others and to ourselves by 'translating' or editing it into other words or modes. When we formalise these processes in speech, writing or print, we call it 'paraphrasing', 'summarising', 'précising', 'abridging', 'making a digest', 'making an abstract', 'epitomising', 'briefing' and so forth. But the important thing to remember is that the processes go on all the time, informally and mentally.

Summary skills are very important at almost every stage of academic writing and research. That is why we have dedicated a whole chapter to them. We use summaries in gathering material – to produce notes on the books we read and the lectures we hear. A plan is a kind of summary or abstract of the larger essay. We use summary skills to paraphrase other people's ideas in the essay itself and we may provide a short digest of a historical event or a sociological theory which provides the context for a book we are analysing. We use abstracting skills for thesis statements. The ability to identify the key points of an argument and to be able to sum up the argument in its entirety are central to academic research and writing and to the important process whereby knowledge is transformed into argument.

In this chapter we will be concentrating on 'summarising', 'précising', 'abridging' and the rest as they are used to produce written texts. Sometimes these processes stick close to the original wording of the source, sometimes not. The strict version of précis, for instance, replaces the author's words as far as possible, while the abridgement replaces them as little as possible. The summary and the paraphrase are midway between these extremes. The writer will very often quote the author's own words or weave them in with his or her own, though some summaries are almost indistinguishable from abridgements. Most of this chapter will be about paraphrase and summary. Paraphrase is unlike summary (and other summarising activities) in one important respect: it does not necessarily shorten its sources, though it *may* do. Summaries, digests, précis, abstracts, epitomes and so forth are always shorter – often considerably shorter – than the originals.

All these skills are intertransferable: if you can do one you can probably do them all. They also have their limitations. Too much emphasis on summary can tend to encourage the view that a writer's meaning can be experienced by extracting a nourishing 'substance' or 'pith' or 'marrow' (like wheat-germ) and that the rest is just a throw-away husk, or it can suggest that an author's style is like a garment that can be removed, revealing the 'body' of the text. Summaries can rub out shades of meaning and the emotive effects of rhythm and emphasis: 'He was soon borne away by the waves, and lost in darkness and distance' (the last sentence of Mary Shelley's *Frankenstein*) is not saying the same thing as 'The Monster vanished into the night'.

Here are definitions of the five terms that are probably most relevant to you, slightly adapted from the complete *Oxford English Dictionary* (*OED*):

- Paraphase: an expression in other words, usually fuller and clearer, of the sense of any passage or text.
- Summary: an account containing the chief points or sum and substance of a matter.
- Précis: a concise or abridged statement, a summary, an abstract.
- Digest: a methodical arrangement, compendium or summary of literary, historical, legal, scientific or other written matter.
- Abstract: a summary or epitome of a statement or document.

Notice that while a paraphrase is clearly different from the rest in that it is not necessarily shorter than the original, the other four definitions overlap. But dictionaries do not tell the whole story of how terms are actually used at any given time. To go further we must look at the history of these terms and some actual examples because each of these forms of summary have evolved for different purposes and therefore have different conventions.

A summary history of paraphrase

Instead of giving you a full version of this next section of the chapter we are going to give you it in note or summary form. This is typical of the kind of summary note-taking we used as we assembled information in preparation for the chapters of this book. It is not suitable for a finished piece of work of course, but it is an important stage in preparing that work.

- Paraphrase (Greek: 'in other words') goes back to the explanation / dissemination of sacred writings and laws by priestly / intellectual / judiciary castes (e.g. Jewish rabbis / Greek philosophers / Roman jurists).
- Reproduction of long manuscripts was expensive before the invention of printing (late 1400s) and long after. Summaries and digests could circulate philosophy, doctrine, biography etc. more cheaply.
- Readers also browse. The early user-friendly author Pliny the Elder (AD 23–79) proudly prefaced his *Natural History* with a contents list for each volume and directed those interested in gender of hyenas or whether seaweed can think to these sections; you don't have to read the whole monumental work. Pliny's device was an early forerunner of the *abstract*.
- Growth of European medieval universities after *c.* 1200 spurred on demand for easily accessed information and keeping lecture-notes. Functioned as study aids and memory aids for oral exams.
- Early modern period to the end of the eighteenth century (*c.* 1450–1800): rise of Western European nation states – emergence of complex commercial and administration systems and growth of secretary class. More demand for report-writing and related skills; growing over next three hundred years. Literacy increases. Latin no longer *the* learned language. Translation into modern languages flourishes. Paraphrase acquires a specialised meaning not in use today: free, creative translation, as opposed to strict, literal translation. John Dryden (1631–1700) called his 'Englishing' of Latin poets (1680) 'paraphrase, or translation with latitude, where the author is kept in view . . . but his words are not so strictly kept in view as his sense' (*OED*). He slyly inserted expressions of his anti-government sympathies.
- Nineteenth century: creation of modern civil services and bureaucracies. Précis serves both – expert skill – formed the basis of a good career. Twentieth century: demand for abridgements, summaries, digests, abstracts etc. grows to keep up with sheer volume of text produced by modern technologies; and will probably continue to do so in the twenty-first century.

Uses of paraphrase and summary

To sum up some of the chief uses and effects of paraphrase and summary:

- *Preservation and recall of information.* Mathematical and chemical formulae, mnemonic systems (artificial memory aids), acronyms, mottoes, slogans are all very specialised forms of summary.
- *Explication and clarification.* These are inseparable from recall. What is incomprehensible is very hard to remember.

- *Time saving*. Reports, digests, abstracts and summaries are always sparing us the trouble of reading through the entire originals, if, of course, they are accurate.
- *Dissemination*. A message can be more easily circulated and repeated if it is brief.
- *Popularisation*. Publisher's blurbs, some kinds of book reviews, retellings of adult classics for children and theatre-programme plot summaries stimulate interest in experiencing the originals, making them seem pleasurable or less formidable.
- *Censorship or misinformation*. All of the above share the same desirable features: conciseness, accuracy, clarity, a clear sense of purpose. But there is also a less worthy function. We give our trust to paraphrases; if we didn't they would be useless. Spin-doctors, advertisers and public relations officers make use of this trust for their own purposes.

ACTIVITY 1:

Choose a recent newspaper article on a controversial subject. Then summarise it for the following different purposes:

- You are briefing your boss, Jane Herrell, for a meeting: what does she need to know about this subject?
- You are writing a 25-word entry for a newspaper about a TV programme on this theme: make the story intriguing.
- You are an investigative reporter with seventy words to 'sell' what you think is a scandal to a senior politician.

In each case you will need to consider: the selection of appropriate detail; the creation of punchy statements; clarity and brevity of expression; the choice of appropriate vocabulary; tailoring the way you write for your specified reader.

The paraphrase

Paraphrase, telling something in your own words without much condensing, is generally used in academic writing to explain what has happened in the plot of a novel or to introduce the views of a critic. A paraphrase is likely to follow closely the sense of the original text, especially in its sequence of ideas or events. It has its place in academic writing but it is a limited place. When it is overused it can cause a number of problems. The most serious problem it can cause is when the paraphrase does not acknowledge its original source. When this is deliberate and substantial it is called plagiarism and is regarded as a serious academic crime. On a much less serious level, when paraphrase is used for excessive knowledge-telling, such as copious plot recounting to 'pad out' an essay, it can seriously weaken the writing because plot description of this kind will almost always act as a substitute for argument. If you have ever found comments on your essays such as 'Too much paraphrase' or 'This is just paraphrase' you will recognise this complaint.

ACTIVITY 2:

Two students write an essay in answer to the following question: 'Write a critical analysis of the following stanza from a poem by Edward Thomas'.

'Tall Nettles' (written c. 1915)

Tall nettles cover up, as they have done
These many springs, the rusty harrow, the plough
Long worn out, and the roller made of stone:
Only the elm butt tops the nettles now.

The first student begins the answer with the following paragraph:

'Tall Nettles', written in 1915, begins with the poet letting the reader know quite definitely that he is in a farmyard looking at nettles. We can tell that he is in a farmyard because of the references to farm machinery but it is an unused farm and we can tell this because there is so much rust. He notices that the weeds have completely overgrown the farm machinery, useless and neglected because the harrow has rusted and the plough is said to be 'long worn out'. The nettles have been growing for a long time, for the poet refers to 'these many springs'. He is amazed and saddened to find that 'the elm butt', maybe a water-butt made out of the wood of the elm tree, is the only thing that is taller than the nettles. He uses simple language. The second stanza ...

The second student begins this way:

This poem about rampant weeds and outworn farm machinery was written in a year when young men were dying on the battlefields of World War I. Through his careful and subtle use of language such as the use of the term 'elm-butt' in line three (the stump of an elm – perhaps cut down to make a wagon?), Edward Thomas enables us to glimpse the battlefield through the rusting machinery of rural England. But does this poem offer images of a dying England, a place of rural depopulation and decay or an escape from war to images of peaceful decay? Are the nettles a hopeful sign of the natural world's vigour and regenerative power or a testimony to the brevity of human memory? In this essay I will explore the ambivalence expressed towards war in Edward Thomas's important poem.

Consider the difference between the two openings and the role that paraphrase plays in that difference.

Let's now consider how paraphrase can be used to summarise an argument. Here is a famous argument for the existence of God made by William Paley in a book called *Natural Theology* published in 1802. It is known as 'The Argument from Design'. The argument appeared in an examination paper with the following instructions: paraphrase the argument, as given below in an adaptation of Paley's words, in one clear paragraph, making sure that you have outlined the conclusion and the premises of the argument, and shown how the premises are intended to justify the conclusion.

> In crossing a heath, suppose I had found a watch upon the ground and it should be inquired how the watch happened to be in that place. When we come to inspect the watch, we perceive that its several parts are framed and put together for a purpose, e.g. that they are so formed and adjusted as to produce motion, and that motion so regulated as to point out the hour of the day. The mechanism being observed, the inference, we think, is inevitable; that the watch must have a maker. In the same way, the universe, which is also made of parts framed and put together so as to produce regulated motion, must have had a maker, whom we call God. (123 words)

The following is a possible response. It is a much re-edited and redrafted version, incorporating points and phrases taken from the papers of students who sat the examination:

> If, Paley says, we found an unfamiliar object, a watch, say, lying on a heath, we would ask ourselves how it came to be there. Examination would show that it has both a mechanism which produces regulated motion and a purpose (telling the time). We could work out that it was made by some unseen person. What applies to a small mechanism can be applied to a larger one: the universe. The universe is like a watch in having parts and motion; the motion, too, following this reasoning, must be regulated (and have some purpose, though Paley does not say so here). It, too, must have an unseen maker. But the invisible maker of the universe, although behaving like a human craftsman, cannot be human, and so must be superhuman. So the existence of a superhuman creator can be deduced from the existence of the universe. (148 words)

This is twenty-five words longer than the original, which is fine for a paraphrase, although usually paraphrases will be the same length or even a little shorter. You notice that certain ideas in the original have been compressed (e.g. 'parts framed and put together' becomes 'a mechanism') but that others are added in order to make the assumptions of the argument more explicit. Some phrasing has been kept, such as 'regulated motion', which there is no point in changing; in any case, although paraphrase means 'in other words' it is normal to use phrases from the original, either embedded or as quotations.

ACTIVITY 3:

Do you think that the paraphrase is just as persuasive as the original, more persuasive or less persuasive? Why? Do you think that the paraphrase is an exact and objective exposition of Paley's argument, or does it betray bias either for or against Paley? Justify your viewpoint.

Paraphrase, as we have said, is of some use in academic writing, but because it tends not to compress it is of limited use. After all, the conclusions of Paley's reasoning might be more relevant than the detail and in a world in which essays have strict word limits, more compressed versions of arguments are usually necessary. It might be necessary therefore to summarise Paley's 'Argument from Design' in one sentence.

ACTIVITY 4:

Read Richard Dawkins's reply to Paley in his book *The Blind Watchmaker* (1986):

> Paley's argument is made with passionate sincerity and is informed by the best biological scholarship of his day, but it is wrong, gloriously and utterly wrong. The analogy between telescope and eye, between watch and living organism, is false. All appearances to the contrary, the only watchmaker in nature is the blind forces of physics, albeit deployed in a very special way. A true watchmaker has foresight: he designs his cogs and springs, and plans their interconnections, with a future purpose in his mind's eye. Natural selection, the blind, unconscious, automatic process which Darwin discovered, and which we now know is the explanation for the existence and apparently purposeful form of all life, has no purpose in mind. It has no mind and no mind's eye. It does not plan for the future. It has no vision, no foresight, no sight at all. If it can be said to play the role of watchmaker in nature, it is the *blind* watchmaker.

> (Dawkins 1986: 5)

Summarise Paley's argument in one sentence. Then do the same for Dawkins's counter-argument.

The summary

The summary has a range of uses similar to the paraphrase, but it generally involves more compression. Clarification comes instead from cutting away material so that the 'chief points' stand out. A lecture may often be an elaborate form of summary, a distillation of much reading. Note-taking during lectures is often a form of secondary summary, though the students of the Irish playwright Samuel Beckett, who had a brief academic career before becoming a writer, had a different experience. According to his biographer, Deirdre Bair, his lectures were delivered with such long pauses between each sentence that students were able to take down every word in long hand! On the other hand, the chief work of Ferdinand de Saussure (1857–1913), one of the founders of modern linguistics, was preserved by his students' summarising skills (though they must have had good memories as well). After his death they were able to expand their notes and reconstruct something like the original lectures.

'Summary' is a very broad and flexible term. As with a paraphrase, there are no set rules as to how much shorter a summary should be than the original, or how far you should write it 'in your own words', any more than there is an answer to the question 'how long is a piece of string?' All depends on the nature of the original, the aim of the summary and what is asked for. So you may, for instance, be asked to summarise the proceedings of a meeting 'in one paragraph'.

ACTIVITY 5:

Here is the Paley passage again, but this time summarised in two sentences:

> The writer supposes that he found a watch upon the ground and noticed that it told the time. This shows that the watch was manufactured, just like the universe, which was manufactured by God. (34 words)

What is inadequate about this summary, considered as a summary, not a paraphrase? Compare this to the summary of Paley's argument you produced earlier.

Summarising helps you to remember and clarify what you have read. When you have finished reading a critical essay or book it is always useful to ask yourself questions such as 'what has this book been about?', 'what has it proved or claimed?', 'what is its argument?' in order to aid your memory. Gradually you should be able to summarise each piece of critical writing that you read in terms of its key arguments. But, as we said earlier, you must always acknowledge the ideas you use from others. Putting it into your own words does not mean that it *is* your own words. If in doubt always acknowledge the idea by giving the reference to the original source of the idea.

Sometimes summaries are bad not in their effects but in themselves. They are just bad *as* summaries. They miss the point of the original or have left out so much that they don't make sense. When you are reading critical texts that offer a survey of key works in the field, don't always assume that the summaries of key texts will be accurate just because they sound authoritative. Most will be, of course, but it's worth reading with a critical eye and remembering that summaries are only selective. It's always better to read the whole book, rather than a summary, but sometimes you need to get a bird's eye view and the summary achieves this very well.

ACTIVITY 6:

Read the following sentence from an affected or 'precious' piece of writing by Bedivere Inskip called *Troubadours, the True, the Bad and the Dour* (1953):

> The delicious idea that European literature originated in the activities of wandering minstrels – Bertrands, Arnauts, Jeffrois, or similarly-named tunesmiths – roaming from one pepperpot-towered castle in Provence to the next, wailfully beseeching their scornful ladies to show great mercy upon them, has long been shown – alas! – to be as insubstantial as those faerie lands of 'far away and long ago'. (61 words)

(Inskip 1953: 27)

This is rather turgid, but the following summary has gone to the opposite extreme.

> The wandering Provence minstrel view of European literature's beginnings is now wrong. (12 words)

This certainly cuts the word spinning, but is knotted up and cryptic. Excessive cutting is a common fault of summarising. Rewrite a summary of the original in order to clarify and condense the original sentence. You have a limit of thirty words.

ACTIVITY 7:

Choose a critical book or essay you have read recently on any subject. Summarise it in one paragraph.

ACTIVITY 8:

This is the third draft of an actual task. It is the opening paragraph of a 5,000-word chapter on Mary Shelley as a Gothic writer which I was asked to contribute to a handbook on the Gothic, aimed at both an academic and general readership. The focus was to be on *Frankenstein* as a Gothic novel, which determined what information was selected. The General Editor advised me that the reader might be supposed to know the plot of *Frankenstein*, though not necessarily very much about Mary Shelley. This was my attempt:

> Mary Shelley was only nineteen when she wrote *Frankenstein* (published 1818), an extraordinary and almost unique achievement for someone of her age. This 'Gothic romance' unleashed onto the world a famous duo: the student of unhallowed arts and the monster whom he creates out of corpses. However, that she should have written a Gothic romance is hardly surprising. She was an avid reader of the genre, and her reading lists record many titles, from *The Monk* to *Hermann of Unna*. The influence of every one of these, to a greater or lesser extent, can be seen on *Frankenstein*. In fact, if one were to attempt to categorise the kind of Gothic to which *Frankenstein* may be said to belong, a fair answer would be that, like its monster, it is a hybrid. Undoubtedly this hybrid quality accounts for the book's seemingly endless capacity to generate diverse interpretations. (148 words)

This was shaping up, but it was still too overblown and unfocused. The final version reduced it to seventy words. See if you can do the same. You will probably find that you use some straight abridgement, but will also have to recast.

The précis

'Précis' and 'summary' are often used interchangeably. The précis, like the summary, is also intended to reduce a passage to its chief points. Nevertheless, they have been and can be distinguished in practice.

The 'précis writer' became a paid bureaucratic post in the early nineteenth century. Précis formed part of the competitive recruitment examination devised in the 1820s by India House (the body which administered Britain's Indian empire from London) and other civil service organisations followed. Schools prepared their students to compete for such posts. In schools and public examinations, précis writing evolved into a very particular formal discipline, with rigid conventions. While there was (and is) no absolute code, in practice the following rules were usually observed:

- *A third of the original.* No more, no less. A short passage of prose (less often poetry) was to be reduced to about a third of its original length (custom sportingly allowed up to five words over the word limit). No idea was to be added and nothing of importance was to be omitted. There was no minimum length, but anything very much below this proportion was almost certain to result in important omissions.
- *Own words.* Any phrase more than three or four words long 'lifted' word for word from the original was regarded as a fault. Even short quotation was discouraged. A précis is not like a modern 'abridgement' in this context, despite the dictionary definition.
- *Continuous writing, not in note form.* The précis must read coherently overall. *It must not be a sequence of disjointed sentences or paragraphs.*
- *'Neutral' style in modern Standard English.* No attempt was to be made to capture the 'flavour' of the original (whereas, as we have seen, a paraphrase and a summary frequently do this). Direct speech was usually put into reported speech.

You can readily see that précis writing has negative features. Here is my shortlist (you can no doubt think of others):

- The one-third length is arbitrary. (To be fair, many précis-writing guides recognised this and showed flexibility.) Passages have tended to be chosen precisely because they lend themselves to being reduced to a third (and sometimes are so boring as to arouse suspicions of having been written for no other purpose!).
- The 'in your own words' rule can encourage pointless verbal substitutions, such as 'the monarch decreed' for 'the king commanded' or two long words instead of three short ones, just to save a word.
- Zest for compression can encourage cryptic, inelegant writing and uncouth word coinages.
- Précis writing tends to encourage a curt, imperious style which is fine for framing safety warnings, as in 'Mind the gap! Stand away from the doors!', but this style can be inappropriately brusque. Tactful, polite phrases such as 'You might like to . . .' 'It might be worth considering . . .' are ruthlessly cut out as 'unnecessary' padding.
- The précis's formal rules, applied without judgement, can encourage 'getting in everything but expressing it more briefly' at the expense of highlighting the most important ideas. Précis-writing tends to encourage trimming off words evenly all round. But sometimes what is needed is to slash larger units ruthlessly and to leave others intact.

By about 1970, British examination boards had moved away from the strict précis. More stress was placed on the student's own judgement about length and coverage. Questions were more liable to be cast in the form of 'Summarise the following in your own words, selecting what you consider to be its most important ideas'. There was less emphasis on 'own words'. Nevertheless, the stern discipline of the précis had its merits as an exercise. Many of the drawbacks listed above really are about its misuse, and misuse of something doesn't discredit its proper use. (For instance, you are not *obliged* to use pompous language.) Among these merits are the following:

- It really does stretch and develop your resources of vocabulary and sentence-framing.
- You train yourself to aim at getting across the sense of the original with scrupulous accuracy and without bias, even if you disagree with it.
- You are continually having to exercise your judgement about what may be usefully omitted. This makes you mentally agile.
- You learn to spot wordy formulaic phrases such as 'the fact that', 'it is the case that', 'it may be possible to' and so on, and to prune these from your own writing.
- Précis writing may no longer land you a secure job in the British Foreign Office at £300 a year with prospects (you would have to go back to the 1830s for that) but its relevance as training for the journalist or the editor or advertising copy-writer is obvious. Think, too, of the following: 'Use no more than one side of A4 paper', 'For the tie-breaker, finish the sentence "Yes! I want a Seychelles holiday because . . ." in no more than 25 words' or 'The Editor regrets that letters of over 400 words are less likely to be published'. It is a skill that can be adjusted to many situations (and it is always easy to relax the 'rules').

ACTIVITY 9:

Shorten these sentences, keeping the original words where there is no reason for altering them. We have offered a possible answer for the first one. See if you can make (or beat) the targets we have set:

> It was with nervousness and foreboding that we awaited the millennium. (11 words; target = 5) [Possible answer: We awaited the millennium apprehensively.]
>
> Dante Gabriel Rossetti had the coffin of his late wife dug up and opened so that he could take out the manuscript notebook containing his poems. (26 words; target = 13 words)
>
> Samuel Johnson could not tell the difference between his right shoe and his left shoe. (15 words; target = 8 words)
>
> All of a sudden, P.B. Shelley uttered a piercing shriek and measured his length on the floor. He had had a hallucination in which he imagined that a woman with eyes instead of nipples was staring at him. (38 words; target = 22 words. There *is* a word meaning 'having eyes in the bosom', *'sternophthalmos'*, but unfortunately it is a classical Greek one. Sorry, not allowed!)

> The first meeting between Sylvia Plath and Ted Hughes was famous for being the occasion on which she attracted his attention by biting him on his cheek. (27 words; target = 17 words)

ACTIVITY 10:

Read this passage from a nineteenth-century history book.

The Sack of Nordhovengar

When Hradicziu entered the luckless city of Nordhovengar, five days after the retreating troops of Charles VII had wreaked their vengeance, his horrified eyes encountered a scene of atrocity, horror and desolation. Not an inhabitant had been spared. The appalling stench of death exhaled from the ruins. Sullen and fattened Pomeranian hounds skulked in the cobbled streets, rending and devouring the putrefying corpses of men, women and even unweaned babes. But what made even Hradicziu's hardened soldiers weep was ocular proof that Charles's army, not content with the customary stabbing, cutting of throats, burning alive and impalement, had devised refinements of cruelty in the means of encompassing death, such as the pen of this historian must refrain from detailing.

(Merriman 1840: 321; 120 words)

Draft a précis of this passage, following the traditional 'rules' of précis writing, trying to use no more than forty words. If you are working in a group, show the other members your draft and see if you can collectively devise a draft or drafts. What has been lost from the passage in turning it into a précis?

ACTIVITY 11:

Can one précis anything? This is an extract from Shylock's speech to the court in Act V of Shakespeare's *The Merchant of Venice*. The justice has asked Shylock why he prefers to take a pound of flesh from Antonio's heart in discharge of a debt instead of the three thousand ducats that he has been offered by the city. This is his reply:

Some men there are love not a gaping pig,
Some that are mad if they behold a cat,
And others, when the bagpipe sings i' th' nose
Cannot contain their urine; for affection,
Master of passion, sways it to the mood
Of what it likes or loathes. Now for your answer:
As there is no firm reason to be rendered
Why he cannot abide a gaping pig,

Why he a harmless necessary cat,
Why he a woollen bagpipe, but of force
Must yield to such inevitable shame,
As to offend, himself being offended:
So can I give no reason, nor I will not,
More than a lodged hate and a certain loathing
I bear Antonio, that I follow thus
A losing suit against him. (109 words)

This was my introduction to précising at school (the lines about the bagpipe were tactfully shortened to 'And others at the bagpipe' or omitted altogether). We had to compress the essential argument of Shylock's reply into thirty-five words. I was mildly amused at treating Shakespeare in this somewhat disrespectful way. One of the difficulties we found was that there was no obvious general term that would cover pigs, cats and bagpipes. Even the model answer we were given chickened out and called them all 'animals'. Not good enough!

Aim at a thirty-word prose précis, beginning 'Shylock replied that...'. What is lost in your précis? Did you find it more or less easy than the passage on the sack of Nordhovengar? Why do you think this was?

The digest and the abstract

Like the précis, these are varieties of the summary. As with most of these terms, they have altered their meaning over time. The long-established American monthly magazine *The Reader's Digest* uses 'digest' to mean both 'compendium' and 'abridgement'. Each number of the magazine offers a sample of writing on a wide range of subjects (medicine, current affairs, people, show-biz, home, teenagers, sex, modern living, the future, etc.), and each piece is usually an abridged reprint of something which has appeared somewhere else. I am using 'digest' here as the term for a particular subspecies of summary, the potted biography or 'the digested read'.

It would be wrong to think of summary and précis as stifling creativity and individuality. As an examination exercise there is little scope for either, but it is a different matter when the skills acquired are applied to an interesting task.

The postcard biography

As an example of what great writers can do with a strict word limit, let us take the British National Portrait Gallery's Postcard Biographies. In the 1920s, the gallery commissioned famous authors of the day each to write a very short biography (approximately seventy words) of a celebrity represented in the collection, the result to be reproduced on the back of a postcard. The mini-biographies vividly (and often controversially) characterised their subjects, while the biographer's distinctive personal style still came through, as here:

> Sprung from country people but insatiably intellectual, George Eliot's early novels are the fruit of happy memory; her later of melancholy thought. Isolated by an ambiguous marriage, extravagantly praised, she early lost vitality and her novels suffered. But she stretched the capacity of fiction, and forced it not only to tell a story and reflect manners but to contain the comment and criticism of a large mind brooding over life.
>
> (Virginia Woolf on George Eliot (1819–1880))

ACTIVITY 12:

Write a postcard biography, keeping to the seventy-word limit, on any well-known figure, using Virginia Woolf on George Eliot as a guide as to content, but without trying to imitate her style. You may use any biography or encyclopaedia or Guide to English Literature to help you gather information.

The digested read

Summarising skills continue to find novel outlets. Below is an example of 'The Digested Read', at the time of writing, a regular feature in the *Guardian*'s supplement *The Editor*. Primarily offered as amusement, 'The Digested Read' claims to run a useful service for busy readers who wish to keep abreast of the best-sellers. Each week, a helpful hack skilfully boils down a book-plot to 400 words, and then offers a digest of the digest. But, while pretending to pander to the culture vultures, the 'Digested Read' is often a tongue-in-cheek cover for a witty evaluative review; it is usually possible to tell whether the summariser is recommending the book or not.

THE DIGESTED READ

Too busy to read the hot books? Let us read them for you
Men are from Mars, Women are from Venus
by John Gray (Thorsons, £9.99), condensed in the style of the original.

John Gray's guide to relationships was published in 1993, but remains a best-seller. Gray has founded the Mars-Venus Institute and the Mars and Venus Counselling Centre, and holds Mars-Venus workshops and Personal Success Seminars. As well as Mars and Venus the video, board game, and compilation album, further titles in Gray's series include Mars and Venus on a Date, Mars and Venus in Love, Mars and Venus in the Bedroom *and, out this week,* Mars and Venus: 365 Ways to Keep your Love Alive. *This is his core message:*

Without the awareness that we are meant to be different, men and women are at odds with each other. Men complain that women want to change them. When a woman loves a man, she forms a home-improvement committee to focus on his personal growth. She thinks she is nurturing him, but he feels controlled. Instead, he wants her acceptance. A man's sense of self is defined through his ability to achieve. To offer a man unsolicited advice is to presume that he does not know what to do, or that he cannot do it on his own.

To feel better, Martians withdraw to their caves. Never go into a man's cave or you will be burned by the dragon! To feel better, Venusians get together and talk openly about their problems. Recognise the validity of her feelings. Men are like rubber bands. When a man loves a woman, periodically, he needs to pull away before he can get closer. Women are like waves. A woman's self-esteem rises and falls like a wave. When her wave crashes, it is time for her emotional housecleaning. In relationships, men pull back then get close, while women rise and fall in their ability to love themselves and others.

To score points with a woman, give her four hugs a day, and give her 20 minutes of unsolicited quality time per day. To score big with a man, instead of expressing disapproval, go into another room to centre yourself and return with a loving heart, and enjoy having sex with him.

Write a Love Letter communicating your anger, sadness, fear and love. Write a Response Letter articulating what you want to hear from your partner. Share the letter with your partner. If a woman does not ask for support, a man assumes she is getting enough. Men are more willing to say yes when they have the freedom to say no.

To keep the magic alive, understand the four seasons of love. Falling in love is like springtime. Throughout the summer of love, we realise that men and women are from different planets, and we have to work at our relationship. The fruits of our labour are reaped in the autumn of love. Then comes winter, a time of reflection and renewal.

And if you really are pressed: The digested read, digested

Men and women are from different planets. A man needs trust, acceptance, admiration and approval. A woman needs care, understanding, respect and reassurance

(Guardian)

ACTIVITY 13:

Write a 400-word Digested Read of a book you have recently read. Then try to reduce it to no more than 25 words. Ask a friend to write a digest of your original 400-word Digested Read too (without seeing yours) and compare the two.

The dissertation abstract

If you write a dissertation, you will almost certainly consult *abstracts* of articles or books and you will usually be required to write your own abstract of your dissertation. Abstracts make you aware of the range of published material on your topic and save you the time of locating a promising title, only to find that it has nothing whatever to do with your subject. For instance, a horticulturalist might think that an article called 'The Puzzling Mimosa' is about the problems of propagating the sub-tropical flowering plant of that name. Actually, it is a literary essay on the fascination of eighteenth-century poets with the mimosa, a plant which appeared to them to have some human feelings (like modesty). An abstract would show this up.

Here are two examples of abstracts from third-year English students' dissertations. The dissertations were of 8,000 words. Both abstracts are excellent in their own ways – concise, attentive to argument and offering a kind of map to the reader.

Abstract 1

This dissertation examines the major themes of entrapment and escape in the poetry of Emily Brontë.

The first chapter discusses the relatively unexplored nature of Brontë's poetry, the encumbrance of Gondal and the escape of the artist herself from her inherited literary models. As an initial step towards independence Brontë's stoical attitude is also examined.

Chapter two considers the changing relationship with the natural landscape. Initially a source of solace from physical and psychological imprisonment, it is elevated to the status of a personal religion. Yet as an external force, it proceeds to adopt a malevolent character, threatening to rob Brontë of her personal liberty.

Chapter three traces the withdrawal from nature and the seeking of a means of release within the self. Brontë celebrates the individual imagination as an alternative existence free from external threat, and undertakes nocturnal visionary experience in order to achieve union with an absolute force.

Yet, as Chapter four explores, this spiritual satisfaction can only be momentary, and thus Brontë recognises the satisfactions offered by death, as a way of escaping imposed identity and reuniting with one's true self. In recapturing the lost harmony with nature there is hope of renewal.

In conclusion, Chapter five focuses on 'No Coward Soul' where all previous tension is transcended and the long sought for liberty is finally accomplished. (220 words)

Abstract 2

This dissertation falls into three parts. It opens with a commentary on Milan Kundera's perception of the novel genre he uses, which is shown to be closely related to the European cultural inheritance that informs his world-view. To set the author's statements on culture and literature in a wider context I have considered his ideas in conjunction with existing critical debates about the nature and function of the novel genre within society, as well as addressing what effect Kundera's own status as a political exile has had on his fiction. Chapter Two, which constitutes the main body of the dissertation, discusses in detail the thinking which underlies Kundera's presentation of Western society in *Immortality*, drawing on earlier works and essays in order to emphasise the clear continuities in the Czech's fictional output. Lastly, and in view of the importance of Kundera's personal standpoint on European culture to his fiction, the dissertation concludes by arguing that criticism is sometimes guilty of ignoring the motivations and purpose of an author, which can lead to literature being misrepresented by critics who are too ready to apply generalising literary paradigms when commenting on a text. (191 words)

ACTIVITY 14:

Analyse the differences between these two styles of dissertation abstract. Which do you prefer and why? Now write an abstract of a recent academic essay of your own in no more than 200 words.

Summary

In this chapter we have examined:

- the use of summary in academic writing and research
- the history and development of paraphrase and précis
- paraphrase
- summary
- précis
- digest and abstracts.

References

Dawkins, Richard (1986) *The Blind Watchmaker*. Harlow: Longman.

Inskip, Bedivere (1953) *Troubadours, the True, the Bad and the Dour*. London: Petite Jaunisse Press.

Merriman, M.M. (1840) *A History of the Great Northern War*, *vol. 6*, London.

Paley, William (1802) *Natural Theology*. London: R. Faulder.

Postcard Biographies (National Portrait Gallery Art & Life Series; pack of twenty-five postcards).

If you suspect that the Inskip and Merriman passages are pastiches from the chapter-writer's imagination . . . you would be right!

CHAPTER 6

Editing skills, or adventures in densely-packed sentences

Rick Rylance

Opening moves

The last thing one settles in writing a book is what one should put in first.

(Pascal)

Editing works in a different time zone from that of composition. It is the last thing you do, but often the first thing that a reader notices. A badly-edited piece is full of errors; it doesn't read easily; it leaves the reader frustrated or irritated, unsure where s/he is going. However wrongly, a poorly edited piece of writing suggests carelessness, a lack of concern for your work, and a lack of consideration for your reader. It suggests you can't be bothered. Your reader therefore sometimes thinks 'nor can I'.

It is sometimes said that in job interviews most candidates fail to get the job within a minute of entering the interview room. There is something about first impressions that puts an interviewer off more than at any other point in the process. You are a stranger, and interviewers can easily mis-understand you; they have no familiarity with your way of conducting yourself and tend to be suspicious because, in the end, they will have to grade you positively or negatively. This is one reason why interviewees should take particular care over the first impressions they give. They provide a platform for your subsequent performance.

The same is true of writing essays. The beginning of your piece goes a long way to establishing the early framework for grading your work: a marker will often form an early impression of whether an essay is likely to be a struggle or a joy to read. But sometimes when you start to write you are not sure where you are going. You are thinking things through as you get underway. Your writing needs to warm up before your best work appears. This is true for virtually all writers at whatever level.

So editing the beginning of your piece after you have completed the whole is especially important. The succinct, considered opening statement that gets the ball rolling smoothly is often actually written *last* for the simple reason that when you begin you don't quite have in focus what it is you are trying to be succinct or considered about. So here is the first set of editing rules:

- Pay particular attention to your opening paragraphs: are they clear and succinct, do they establish a clear direction for your argument?
- Ensure you engage with the question you are answering early, explicitly and directly.
- Expect to lose *at least* 80 per cent of your original opening, however laborious it was to compose.
- Beware of formula beginnings which are easily composed, but always read like clichés (you don't go into your interview wearing second-hand clothes that don't fit you or the occasion).
- Beware of over-complex first sentences – they alienate your reader, who is looking for a smooth introduction to your response to the question, your line of thought and the development of your argument.

Below are two illustrations of problems frequently encountered at the start of essays, with suggestions about how you might edit them to produce a more welcome result. Here is the first example: the opening sentence that leaves you uninspired:

Example A, Version 1

Over the last decade reports and opinions about the perceived problem of declining standards of literacy amongst undergraduates have been raised by employers and the press time and again, and have caused considerable heated discussion in all circles among teachers, university managers, educationalists and politicians as well as bosses and writers of editorials.

This sentence, which is not technically a bad one in so far as it hangs together in an orderly way, nonetheless makes a poor beginning. It has no strong, sprightly rhythm to invite the reader into the essay. It's too long, and by the time you've waded through it, you feel the relatively simple ideas it conveys have not been worth the mental effort of sorting it out and keeping pace with it. So let's try a different version:

Example A, Version 2

Over the last decade, newspapers and employers have frequently claimed that standards of literacy amongst undergraduates are declining.

This doesn't set the world on fire either, but it is succinct, easily understood, relatively confident and breezy. It establishes a platform for what comes next, and the reader can move on quickly and easily. Also, it doesn't lose any of the significant content of the much longer version 1. So, try to gain your reader's attention with a strong opening, and follow the second set of editing rules:

- Be direct.
- Write with the least complication possible.
- Look for a good quote, startling fact or other attention-grabber to begin.
- Be clear about your meaning and the subject you are dealing with.
- Set up a proposition which can begin an argument. In the case of version 2, the writer could move forward either to agree or disagree with the idea that standards are declining, or s/he might take a more measured view. Whatever your choice, you should signal your line of argument early and clearly.
- If you are struggling with a revision, scrap the lot and start again.

The second example needs a drastic edit. This solution is, alas, a common one for the beginnings of essays. Fortunately, it's one which is usually less necessary later. But there is a general rule here: sometimes, in editing, it is best to start a paragraph again rather than try to repair a bad job. If a paragraph doesn't fit the shape of your essay, just put it aside and write one that does. You can trim and tinker with something that can't work until you drive yourself insane. Think: what is the essential point I am trying to make? Then say it: simply. Forget the fine phrases you've already written if they are getting in the way. If they are that fine, you can use them another time.

Example B, Version 1

Discuss the major innovative achievements of the English Romantic poets.

The Romantic period in English literature was a time of great change. There were upheavals in the political world following the French and American Revolutions and, at home, there was popular distress and agitation. Many objected to what was perceived as a harsh government response to popular anger and protest. People were caught in huge economic and social changes, moving from the countryside to the towns, and the first industrial cities began to be developed. There was considerable poverty, which was visible to all writers. The so-called Romantic poets came in two generations: Blake, Wordsworth and Coleridge in the first, and Byron, Shelley and Keats in the second. In addition, many less well known or widely studied figures, such as John Clare, Robert Burns, Anna Laetitia Barbauld and Helen Maria Williams, are often grouped with the Romantics. Important prose writers include Scott, Ann Radcliffe, Hazlitt, Mary Shelley, Jane Austen and Mary Wollstonecraft. The influence of Romanticism can be seen in the work of many Victorian writers, such as Ruskin, Tennyson and Browning, and even in modern figures such as D.H. Lawrence. Many Romantic poets wrote about nature in original ways which have since become very familiar.

What is wrong with this as an opening? It is not factually inaccurate, and it briefly characterises a complex set of developments. It displays a range of information, and places the Romantics loosely in a generalised historical context. It engages the question too, in a way, because it sets a framework for understanding the changes the Romantic poets introduced. *But*: it fails to engage the question directly enough; it doesn't offer a clear line of argument to be developed: it reduces complex developments to rather tired, obvious and over-simplifying phrases which are too generalising and analytically lightweight; and it provides an overload of information which is not very relevant to the question being addressed.

In short, it is over-complicated, dull and predictable. Your marker will have read it many times before and will groan. These groans can be heard at some distance. A version of this paragraph, in fact, could be the beginning of almost any essay on the Romantics, or – with the historical names changed – any essay on anything. I've seen versions of it in essays on medieval, Renaissance, Victorian and modern literature which all begin 'The X period was a period of great change . . .', because all periods are. This opening might just be OK at the beginning of a rather unexciting book where there will be space later for more original ideas or information. But in an essay, with only a handful of words to play with, it's wasteful. It is telling the reader/marker what s/he has heard lots of times before instead of what s/he wants to hear, which is *your* ideas and arguments as they emerge from *your* reading and thinking. Anyway, this hand-me-down beginning starts on an impossible task: how could anyone usefully or interestingly characterise a whole literary and historical period in a few sentences? It will always be sucked into cliché, stereotype or a puddle of unnecessary information.

Nonetheless, it is sometimes useful to write like this, not because of the result, but because it gets you going towards the good stuff. What you should never do, however, is let it stand. This is what editing can do, usually after you have completed the rest of the essay. Editing cuts away unnecessary clutter, false starts and poor writing – and all of us produce enough of this.

The paragraph might be reduced to the following:

Example B, Version 2

The Romantic poets responded to their changing times in a variety of ways. This essay will focus on four themes and examine work by Blake, Wordsworth, Keats and Shelley. These themes are: . . .

This too is unoriginal, but it is short and serviceable. Any other information – about the political upheavals for instance – should then be offered as you discuss particular works where it will have an immediate point and context. Better still, however, might be a different tactic altogether.

Example B, Version 3

The major English Romantic poets made important innovations in both literary technique and subject matter. Living in a period of rapid economic change and social upheaval, their innovative verse reflected a culture wishing to define new interests and new ways of expressing itself. Consider the opening to this famous poem by Blake from *Songs of Innocence and of Experience* (1794):

> Tyger! Tyger! burning bright
> in the forests of the night,
> what immortal hand or eye
> could frame thy fearful symmetry?
> ('The Tyger' in Blake 1979: 49)

What is new in this poem is not only a new attitude to the natural world, but a new way of expressing that attitude. There is drama and violence in this poem, and the natural world inspires a sense of, at once, awe, alarm and celebration which is communicated by fresh techniques. There is immediate action and vitality conveyed in daringly direct and challenging language. There is also a willingness to probe and interrogate rather than simply repeat traditional ideas. Thus, each stanza ends with an unanswered question. The world portrayed here is new, energetic and full of exotic life and ideas which cannot immediately be understood by reference to old concepts. My argument in this essay will be that the new modes of experience that the Romantic poets discovered cannot be separated from their new ways of writing. To illustrate this, I will examine four topics that preoccupied them: the depiction of the natural world, the condition of the poor, love and sexual desire, and doubt and uncertainty. I will provide illustrations of these from work by Blake, Wordsworth, Keats and Shelley.

The next paragraphs – on the natural world – could then pick up on the ideas introduced by reference to 'The Tyger'.

This new introduction could also be edited down (you might try it yourself). But it is focused, detailed, and emerges straight from a reading of Blake's poem. It also establishes a structure and direction for the argument to come (a thesis statement), and a way towards the next and subsequent paragraphs.

So the third set of editing rules is:

- Focus on the question, not on bits and pieces of 'background'.
- Indicate the way you see the essay developing.
- Don't waste time with second-hand generalisations.
- Get your discussion underway as quickly as possible.
- Be as specific and detailed as possible, especially with reference to your reading in the primary sources.

Poor word choice, the dangly sentence and the mental mouthful

Throughout your work, your sentences should be clear and efficient. This does not mean that you must use a pedestrian prose which plods along in a monotone. You should try to vary syntactical structures, to express observations or ideas vividly, and to reach for an ambitious, but apposite, vocabulary. But the creation of a good style often depends on the careful polishing of your language at the editing stage. A dramatic effect is useless if it obscures the basic meaning, and few writers can achieve good style without practising the basics first. The editing of your writing at this stage should ensure basic clarity, the effective structuring of ideas and the correct deployment of supporting evidence and illustration. From that, even better writing will grow.

Word choice is a key issue, and you need to work on it with a diction-ary and thesaurus to hand. You have to ensure that you fully understand the precise meanings of the words you use (it's surprising how many words we think we understand which surprise us when we finally look them up), and that those you choose do, indeed, convey accurately the meaning you intend. Markers will point out errors when they occur, though it is common for poor word choice to create such obscurities in meaning that no clear alternative can be suggested. The editing stage should be the point at which you ask yourself: 'am I confident about the meaning of this word or phrase?' If not, look it up, and change it if necessary. (It might be worth checking some others, too, to make sure you are sure.) This pro-cess will be tiresome at first, like checking your spelling. But, like learning good spelling, the process will accelerate and the benefits will be tangible. Enlarging your vocabulary, and making sure that words are used accurately, will do as much as anything to improve your writing by giving it variety and precision.

Faulty word choice is hard to illustrate helpfully because, by its nature, it is case-specific. But the following are examples of another common prob-lem: sentences which fail to convey clearly the ideas they contain. They make the reader's job difficult, but they also make the writer's job difficult too. If you lose your reader by obscurity of expression, faulty structure, or poor word choice, it's hard work getting his/her attention back.

Version 1 of the following sentences present problems. They might be too long or too straggly to make a strong, meaningful impact. They might be muddled or confusing in their meanings. Version 2 offers an edited version (one amongst several that may be possible). Often the sentences have been shortened or reorganised; sometimes they require something to be added to make a meaning clear; and the punctuation has sometimes been changed.

But basic meanings have not been altered. The principles are simple and fairly obvious, though putting them into practice – especially on your own work – frequently isn't. It is generally true that editing other people's prose is easier than editing your own. This is because you are often too close to your own text, and tend to read over your own ingrained habits and mannerisms. So a good tactic might be to organise working at this stage with others, editing bits of their work. As well as gaining immediately from others' improvements to your writing, you will learn about working on language from your efforts on their behalf. Editing is all about learning to handle language confidently and efficiently.

Example A

Version 1

This exposes a flaw in the idea that individuals have choice and that choice always enables the individual to determine their own future and development when encumbered by a family and the responsibility which that entails coupled with unemployment.

Version 2

This exposes a flaw in the idea that individuals have choice and that choice always enables the individual to determine their own development. This proves not to be the case when individuals are unemployed, or encumbered by a family, or both.

Example B

Version 1

This idea could be overlaid on Hamm's storytelling to create meaning and self-identity. His parable has no real meaning which is a fictionalising of everything, with all its alternatives of weather and allusions to other stories, is his way of engaging with something, even if it is a fiction. However, this too is a form of entrapment because it is fiction and creates a sense of claustrophobia and not liberation.

Version 2

The idea is connected to Hamm's storytelling, which he uses to create meaning and an identity for himself. But his parable is pure fiction and has no real meaning. Its inconsistencies (even with respect to the weather), and allusions to other well-known stories, such as Good King Wenceslas, suggest that real happenings are not being remembered. As a result, it conveys a sense of claustrophobia, of a man caught within his own mind-games, and not a liberation.

Example C

Version 1

Even though he is immobile Hamm has the power of entrapment over the other characters he says to Clov: ...

Version 2

Even though he is immobile, Hamm has the power to trap others. He says to Clov: ...

ACTIVITY 1:

Here is another example of a sentence which should never have seen the light of day in this form (it is the beginning of the essay and so is doubly depressing to read). When you have read it, re-write it in a way that is useable.

Since the controversy surrounding the publication of *The Satanic Verses* ten years ago, the writing of Salman Rushdie has taken a backstep in that it has not been valued or considered in the manner that it deserves to do so as a work of art.

ACTIVITY 2:

Here is a more complicated example, but the editorial principles remain the same. Turn this sentence into more effective writing.

One of the effects of using documentary techniques to create a sense of realism within the film, was to shatter the myths of the all-supporting Welfare State and the idea of close-knit, nuclear, working-class families in the post-war modern Britain and to show that the Welfare State did not create equality for all and young people who were attempting self-determination sometimes got it wrong.

The topic of the sentence arrives too late

Sometimes sentences lack clarity because they make the reader wait for their real subject matter. In version 1 the 'meat' of this sentence doesn't arrive until the last moment:

> **Version 1**
>
> Children entering secondary school since 1990 (when the National Curriculum came into effect) were perceived as having declined in terms of reading skills and general literacy.

In the edited version, the point at issue is more immediately apparent:

> **Version 2**
>
> The reading skills and general literacy of children entering secondary school since the introduction of the National Curriculum in 1990 were perceived as having declined.

Keep your verbs active and your sentences short

Too many essays are written in the passive voice. The passive voice is used in English to emphasise the thing done rather than the doer. It is thus a rather impersonal construction, and (as its name suggests) tends to be rather unassertive. By contrast, the active voice is inclined to sound sharper, brisker, more decided.

The passive voice is created by putting the verb *to be* into the same tense as the active verb, and then adding the past participle of the active verb. Here is a basic example:

> Active voice: *Critics argue that...*
> Passive voice with agent: *It is argued by critics that...*
> Passive voice without agent: *It is argued that...*

Some people write habitually in the passive voice for reasons that are obscure (perhaps they lack confidence in making assertive statements, or perhaps they were schooled that way). But persistent passive constructions change the tone of an essay quite markedly, making it more awkward and diffident. They also consume more words. In the example above, the active construction saves just three words, which in itself is neither here nor there. But it is half the length of the first passive construction, and this can make a significant difference multiplied over an essay as a whole.

Sometimes passive constructions are defensible, for instance when no one in particular is cited as a source or agent (e.g. 'It is sometimes claimed that...'). But by and large it is better to avoid the passive and go for the active voice. If you find yourself writing passively habitually, or even sporadically, the change can be made simply and effectively at editing stage. Cumbersome sentences can become crisper and shorter, and be assertively trained.

The unrolling flannel

Sometimes decent ideas are lost because they are expressed too hesitantly, or the point is so over-embellished that it loses its significance. It is as though the writer, lacking the confidence to give the idea its head, hides it behind a curtain of words, or so thoroughly qualifies it that its core evaporates. It is OK to feel unsure about an idea (writers often do); but there are direct ways of expressing this which don't drain the idea of all its life. Trust your reader: if the idea's OK it will survive, but if you are going to wrap it up so it can barely be seen, it's really not worth bothering with anyway. It is the editor's task to ensure this doesn't happen. In version 1, the idea gets lost in a wordy mist.

Version 1

By contrast, Fay Weldon presents contemporary culture and society in an almost fairytale style, but she adds to this subtle negative undertones so that the idea does not fully emerge and leaves the reader confused. The fairytale is not childish, and in places uses very adult ideas and language, but the reader is conscious of it nonetheless. By her development of the character of Ruth, Weldon conveys her appalled dismay in a tongue-in-cheek manner at society. But these ideas are difficult to describe accurately and are not always to be found on every page.

There are several problems here. The first sentence is too long and contains too many ideas at once. These ideas are in tension with each other so the argument as well as the syntax becomes confusing. The writer is trying to convey the very sensible thought that an adult writer like Fay Weldon can exploit fairytale motifs and ideas in her fiction, but that her adult themes and knowing readership complicate the use of these considerably. These two ideas should be kept separate, and might be articulated in separate sentences. The idea is also short of illustration or evidence. Often, difficult concepts or ideas are clarified by the use of an apt illustration. Finally, the tension between the various ideas emerges as a kind of oxymoron towards the end. An oxymoron is a mixing of unexpected qualities that do not usually go together (like bitter-sweet). Here, 'appalled dismay' and 'tongue-in-cheek' is an unlikely combination (though not an impossible one).

ACTIVITY 3:

Rewrite this passage in a more effective form. The novel referred to is Weldon's *Life and Loves of a She-Devil* (1983).

Unruly syntax

Syntax can tangle like wool or spaghetti; it can develop a life of its own like Frankenstein's monster; it can betray you into unintended meanings like a dream. In editing, be alert not just to awkwardnesses and confusions introduced by poor syntactical control, but also to unfortunate meanings or implications. The following are two real examples of notices put on classroom doors to inform students that a class has had to be postponed:

> Dr Smith will not be able to take his seminar today as he cut his foot while shaving. The German Reformation has been cancelled due to illness.

And some car-insurance claims keep office staff amused on quiet days:

> The guy was all over the road. I had to swerve a number of times before I hit him.
> I pulled away from the side of the road, glanced at my mother-in-law, and headed over the embankment.
> I had been driving for forty years when I fell asleep at the wheel and had an accident.

Public notices, because of the need to be very brief, are notoriously prone to double meanings: for example, 'Refuse to be put in this bin' or 'Way Out'. 'Pick Your Own' also sounds strange if imagined as a grumpy response to a request to pick someone else's.

More usually, however, tangled syntax just creates the impression of confusion and carelessness:

> The imagery Weldon uses to describe the transformation Ruth undergoes, is almost gothic and connects Ruth to Frankenstein's monster, by having her body rebuilt.

Or:

> As such the world becomes absurd and meaningless and it is from this absurdity and meaninglessness that individuals are therefore free.

Here, absurdity and meaninglessness are embodied. Does the sentence mean that individuals are free *from* absurdity and meaninglessness, or free *because of* absurdity and meaninglessness? Note too the ugly, unnecessary repetition of the phrase.

The knotty proposition gets knottier

Complex ideas need simple explanations. As a rule, the more difficult the concept, the more patient must be the account of it. If the idea you wish to convey is complex, it will make its own demands, so avoid making things unnecessarily difficult by your complicated sentences. For example,

Version 1

The realist text is on the whole committed to secure portraits of character, whereas the postmodern text firmly conforms to the abolition of humanist values, as it believes them to be illusory.

This might be re-written as:

Version 2

The realist text is committed to uncomplicated portraits of character, whereas the postmodern text attacks humanist values believing them to be illusory.

However, just as it is sometimes necessary to produce a weak opening to an essay before you can go back and write a strong and incisive one, it is sometimes useful to write your account of a complex idea spontaneously just as it arrives, and then edit it into shape. You need to search for the right form of words; they rarely come on cue. Here is a fourth set of editing rules, relating to the communication of complex ideas:

- Use short sentences containing one or at most two propositions.
- Keep the syntax straightforward.
- Make sure there is an orderly progression of points each of which is neatly self-contained.
- Keep ideas and evidence or illustrations apart in separate sentences, or even paragraphs.
- Always resist the temptation to add embellishments to an explanation of a complicated idea; they usually make a mess. Give just enough for your purposes, no more. The same applies to the use of examples: keep them short and simple, and make sure they illustrate what you say they illustrate.

- If you want to enter reservations about the idea you are explaining, do it separately when your explanation is over. Don't mix together an explanation of an idea and a criticism of it – this always creates confusion.

The dead hand of metaphor, cliché and colloquialism

Clichés and jargon are never any use, and should always be eliminated by an editor. The stock phrases of journalism and everyday life (e.g. 'There's a cloud on the horizon', 'ongoing', 'on hold' – indeed virtually anything beginning with 'on'), the clichés of essay writing itself ('Thus we can see that', 'In conclusion we might say'), and the dead metaphors of television reporting ('At the end of the day') should all be ruthlessly exterminated from your writing. There is always a better way of saying it, always a better word to be chosen, and you'll find most of them in a decent thesaurus. Cliché always devalues your idea; always creates the impression of a commonplace thought; always suggests that you can't be bothered to think the issue through or find a more interesting way of saying something, and that you are happy to be trite and obvious. Sometimes, the use of cliché can floor your purpose entirely, no matter how sincere you are in your intentions. A legendary complaint to the BBC, about a programme on contraception, included this sentence: 'I did not expect to have condoms thrust down my throat at that time of the evening'.

Original metaphors, on the other hand, can be very telling indeed. But they are extremely difficult to use effectively for an inexperienced writer. You should ensure they don't fall back into clichéd familiarity, and that they really do illustrate the point you are making. Dramatic metaphors can be distracting as well as illuminating.

Finally, beware of the mixed metaphor, especially the mixed, clichéd metaphor (clichéd metaphors are often hard to spot because they embed themselves unconsciously like viruses).

ACTIVITY 4:

Count the contradictory metaphors – and the confusions in expression – in this short example from a real essay:

> To conclude, it is clear that Loach, Plath and Hughes use very different backdrops to underline issues of cultural and social significance. However, they all use the same route to win their ends. They all use the family, and the complex relationships that exist within this structure, as a vessel to raise these issues.

Now rewrite this as plain prose.

ACTIVITY 5:

The following passages also illustrate some of the dangers in the glib use of cliché and colloquialism. Often these go hand in hand with rather superficial or generalised commentary in the essay as a whole. Rewrite these in a more effective form.

> 'April is the cruellest month' (T.S. Eliot, *The Waste Land*): a conventional poet would usually have April as the first month of spring and therefore a time for renewal and growth. It is clear from the off that Eliot will not provide us with any clear-cut, easily defined optimism, the old poetical associations are off limits.

> The First World War looms over this period like a black cloud and had an unprecedented effect on virtually all spheres of society and culture, forcing all people – priests, plumbers, poets and politicians alike – to reconsider the values they had once taken for granted. Perhaps H.D. [the poet Hilda Doolittle] was calling for those who chose, as many did, to view World War One as a 'jolly good wheeze' to see that it was all too real a destructive force equivalent to that of a hurricane.

ACTIVITY 6:

Here is a piece of metaphorical writing from a history book. It uses metaphor to try to convey quite complex ideas vividly in order to make the argument and the issues stick in the mind. First read it through and identify the metaphors being used. The writer, Norman Davies, is discussing the relative advantages of specialist historians who work on localised projects, and those who try to synthesise the broader picture.

> It would now seem, therefore, that the specialists may have overplayed their hand. There has always been a fair division of labour between the industrious worker bees of the historical profession and the queen bees, the *grands simplificateurs*, who bring order to the labours of the hive. There will be no honey if the workers take over completely. Nor can one accept that the broad outlines of 'general history' have been fixed for all time. They too shift according to fashion: and those fixed fifty or a hundred years ago are ripe for revision. Equally, the study of the geological strata of history must never be divorced from doings on the ground. In the search for 'trends', 'societies', 'economies', or 'cultures', one should not lose sight of men, women, and children.

> > (Davies 1974: 4)

Do you think the metaphors are effective – that is, do they convey the ideas succinctly and vividly? Do you think the way the metaphor changes helps or confuses the issue? Is it 'mixed', or are the metaphors kept sufficiently distinct? (This, by the way, is a matter of opinion rather than right or wrong.) Having considered these issues, you should try to rewrite the passage in plain, un-metaphorical prose. Assess which version you find most effective as a way of conveying the main ideas.

Sometimes metaphors can bring rewards not just of a vivid, crystallising image to convey an argument, but gains of real economy and a sense of drama. Consider the following pithy paragraph:

> Gorbachev's role, though honourable, has been exaggerated. He was not the architect of East Europe's freedom; he was the lock-keeper who, seeing the dam about to burst, decided to open the floodgates and let the water flow. The dam burst in any case; but it did so without the threat of violent catastrophe.
>
> (Davies 1997: 1123)

It would be difficult to see how this summary judgement could be conveyed at all – let alone more effectively – by a more circumspect and pedestrian prose style. (Whether it is a *true* judgement, of course, is a different issue.)

The 'totally' syndrome (or 'the redundant modifier')

A common habit in poorly written academic prose is the overuse of 'redundant modifiers'. Redundant modifiers are adjectives or adverbs which are routinely added though they mean little and add nothing to the impact of phrases or sentences. They are the equivalent of the repetitive use of phrases such as 'basically', 'you know', 'like' or 'as such' in speech. They, too, should be edited to destruction. The most common are probably 'totally' and 'completely', as in the following example taken from a real essay:

> *Cathy Come Home* is a totally bleak portrait of postwar Britain and conveys social and cultural problems completely clearly. In complete contrast, Samuel Beckett's *Endgame* is totally unrealistic. *Endgame* is unsettling and ambiguous. Beckett defamiliarises us with his ability to create situations which are totally unfathomable.

Not the least of the problems with 'totally' is that situations in life are rarely so absolute. The use of the word can also create silly contradictions for essay writers. This one describes Beckett's situations as 'totally unfathomable', but writes 1,000 words about them. What is really meant, of course, is simply that they are frequently unusual and difficult to understand at first. Other words commonly used in this way are 'basically', 'incredibly' (as in 'incredibly realistic', which is actually a contradiction) and 'horrific'.

Editing the content

We have so far concentrated largely on the formal aspects of editing – on sentence construction, word choices, forms of expression, the need to get rid of surplus words, and so on. But clearly this is only one dimension of your essay.

It is difficult to give general advice about editing the content of your work because content is so diverse and particular to individual topics and questions. But in all cases, when you read through your work, you should look especially at the following:

- Do I answer the question *explicitly*? It is a good tactic to make sure, especially in the early stages of an essay, that your reader is told clearly how the material you address is relevant to the question.
- Is there any irrelevance: i.e. are all the materials you discuss, and the points you make, consistently shown to be relevant to the question asked?
- Are there any repetitions?
- Are the points connected together logically and coherently in developing your argument?
- Are the points supported by enough appropriate illustration or evidence? (Remember also that huge amounts of illustration and evidence can easily become repetitious.)
- When you quote, do you discuss what you have quoted, or do you leave it to the reader to work out the point of your quotation?

It is worth bearing in mind that the need to lose words from your early draft sharpens your sense of matters such as repetition, relevance, and the just proportion of illustration and evidence.

Endings

Many formal conclusions to essays are a waste of time, even though generations of teachers have told us that they are necessary. Those that begin with some version of the cliché 'In conclusion we might see that' usually add nothing of value. They tend only to repeat what has already been said, often in formulaic or generalised terms. It is thus a dispiriting way of ending an essay.

Nonetheless, you do need some means of bringing your essay to a close because it shouldn't just halt. It is much better, therefore, to end your previous paragraph with a more upbeat and conclusive line or two, than to waste a third of a page on this sort of thing:

> **Version 1**
>
> Thus we can indeed see that the Romantic period was one of great change and innovation which introduced many new ideas and techniques into English Literature. All of the poets discussed in this essay contributed to this process. Wordsworth described nature in a new way; Blake addressed the condition of the London poor; Keats and Shelley wrote poems describing the heartache of human aspiration and the joy of physical and intellectual pleasure. It was truly a very rich period of writing.

This is quite elegant. It is also pointless. It would gain you no marks, and might lose you one or two for unprovoked drivelling.

It would be much better if (for the sake of argument) the paragraph had included a discussion of Blake's 'The Tyger', to round off the essay on an upbeat note.

> **Version 2**
>
> Each stanza of Blake's poem ends with an unanswered question. The major innovations of the Romantics were to unsettle expectations and to question established beliefs and ways of writing. 'The Tyger' is, thus, typical of the period's best verse.

This, at least, is short. Do stop before you waffle. Or if you waffle, don't do it in public. Edit it out.

Formal conclusions only earn their keep if the argument of the essay requires that a debate be resolved, or a complex discussion, or complicated material, needs to be summed up. If you use a formal conclusion – and it's fine to use a good one – make sure that

- it adds something and doesn't just repeat what has already been said
- it is focused (you might use a short, new quotation to pull things together, for instance)
- it resolves or summarises a debate or argument when this has not previously been done.

Also, if you are concluding, signal that you are doing so explicitly (e.g. 'There are clearly strong arguments both for and against such-and-such . . .'), but be brief, and try to add something fresh and lively.

The following is an example of a weak ending:

> We have seen that editing is an essential part of the writing process, and a practised expertise in its techniques improves essay writing all-round. There are numerous ways in which good editing brings benefits, not the least of which are . . .

Is anyone still awake?

Cutting back to the word limit

It is hard to bring a draft to exactly the right number of words. Few can do this instinctively or regularly, and most need to write in excess and then cut back. This is *not* a disadvantage. When you are editing your work to reduce it, you have a further incentive to sharpen all sorts of aspects of it and avoid, for example, irrelevance, repetition and prolixity. There are many different ways of undertaking this task but, whatever tactics you use, it is important to do it in a planned and systematic way. Do not just hack away at your text. You can usually preserve all your best ideas by trimming.

This example is from a recent academic article for inclusion in a book of essays. It illustrates my standard practice and I find it works for me. As usual, I wrote too much – about 2,000 words above a word limit of 7,000. I therefore had to reduce drastically what I had written. I have learnt to live with this side of my writing. If you can write closer to the target you can save yourself a lot of grief.

I looked, first, for material which I'd thought interesting when I wrote it, but which on reflection appeared not so good, or a sideline from the main argument. I removed this, about three or four paragraphs in all. I then calculated how many words remained, subtracted the number of words I had been allowed for my article, and divided what was left by the number of pages I had written. This gave me an average number of words I needed to lose per page to meet my target. If I recall, the figure was about 45. A double-spaced, typed page carries about 350 words, so 45 is about 13 per cent. This doesn't sound a lot, but it is when you are cutting into your own prose.

The advantages of this technique are that it is methodical, and that psychologically it sets achievable targets. A number like 2,000 is too distant. You need to work closer to numbers that are meaningful in terms of lines that contain 12–15 words each. I keep a tally at the bottom of each page to keep a check on progress.

Not all pages, of course, will allow you to cut 45 words, but some allow you to cut more, as in the example here. The important thing is to maintain progress near the average to get to the target. The other important thing to remember is that most cuts are a positive benefit to what you write. They make your writing clearer, more direct and more succinct. Making sensible cuts also benefits the structure. It brings out the main shape and direction of your argument, gets rid of redundant or distracting material, and removes over-leisurely or lazy phrasing. It makes you ask hard questions about the relevance of what you have written, as well as its effectiveness.

I find this work tiring. I can't do more than a few pages at a sitting. If I stay longer, I stop looking objectively at what is there and read with it instead of against it. I also find that I have to struggle harder with two common enemies: delusive admiration for what I've written, and (much more common) disgust at the foolishness and ugliness of it. You have to try to set

Figure 3

Bradley held to a theory of memory congruent with his overall stance, though at first sight it appears a little unsettling. He starts from two propositions. The first is that human memory has nothing to do with what he calls 'basal' mechanisms such as the reflex arc in physiology or primitive psychological routines of habit formation. Memory, for Bradley, is a high-order, late-acquired phenomenon which is independent of the mechanisms in which it is grounded in more materialist theories.

The second, more startling foundation of Bradley's theory is his proposition that memory is radically unreliable as a recollection of the past. He argues that memory is not a simple retrieval of past mental states or contents, but an ideal construction made in present consciousness. He argues that acts of memory, he avers, although they have some constitutive relationship to past experience, are given shape and significance by present interests, that is, in the continuity of the self towards the future. In Bradley's schema, the mind continually posits to and for itself an 'ideal identity' between past and present which is future-oriented. We remember forwards, he arrestingly puts it, not backwards. Past experience nourishes the process of organisation and actual events therefore have a 'necessary' – though unspecified – relationship to present constructions (this prevents, among other consequences, a damaging epistemological relativism), but they cannot be thought to have a separate, independent existence. The arbitrative and consistent authority always lies in the present.

Bradley's theory of memory is a good illustration of the direction idealist psychological theory took in its opposition to the new materialist psychology. Because it opposes historical forms of explanation, at personal, social and biological levels, the events of the past can have no distinctive ontological status, and Bradley therefore attempts no genetic explanation of the faculty of memory either in terms of its origins in the nervous system or in repertoires of learnt behaviour. The independence and concomitant status of the higher faculties within the causal and

both aside in all editing tasks. It is one reason why editing other people's work is usually much easier.

Chapter 5 offers valuable advice on how to prune your material. What is reproduced here in Figure 3 is a page of my own self-editing. It is from an essay called 'Twisting: Memory from Eliot to Eliot' (Rylance 2000) about changing conceptions of memory from the time of George Eliot to that of T.S. Eliot.

Editing in the 'real world'

Editing isn't merely an academic exercise. It's a life skill for many people. It aids written communication generally, and is an essential part of everyday work for countless numbers of people working in journalism, broadcasting, publishing, advertising, public relations and services, teaching and any industry that requires the rapid transmission of accurate information. The world's biggest publishing concerns are not the visible paperback imprints (which are relatively tiny), but the big computer companies.

Editing is crucial in the accelerated world of high finance where fast knowledge, received and used in seconds, can make fortunes. It is so crucial, indeed, that there are several major businesses in the world, worth billions of pounds, who do little else but transmit financial data and stories in microseconds over the internet from all parts of the inhabited planet. Editing is crucial to this process because it takes competitive humans in financial markets much longer to read a story than it does for it to zoom from Warsaw to Washington. The text arrives instantly, but it has to be accurate and quickly and easily absorbed by busy readers. In this world, people are sacked for straggly sentences and unrolling flannel.

Here is an example of a story that might be transmitted on a large international financial information network. The story itself is fictional, but is based upon one sent by a Russian bureau office about a northern European business. It is in English, note, because that is the language of international finance (as it is of computing, academic and commercial science and air traffic control). There are two versions of the same story. There is an unedited one (labelled Version 1) written by a Norwegian journalist and based upon a company press release. Then there is an edited one (labelled Version 2) written by a British editor working in Moscow (who is an English graduate, as it happens).

The details of the story are not our concern. This is the small fry of financial news – though it could be hugely important to a local economy – and I doubt any fortunes would be made from it. The important thing to observe is the process that occurs from one version to the next, for the principles are the same as in your essays: the creation of straightforward, lucid sentences written in an appropriate register, a well-organised, streamlined delivery of information which is as free of arcane detail as possible, and sequential, logically arranged paragraphs. (Such companies develop a distinctive house style with rules governing the presentation of facts, the order of information presented, the use or misuse of key words, even the ideal number of lines in a paragraph – four, as it happens.) It is worth bearing in mind that the story – had it been real – would have been composed and edited in minutes, not hours, and that it would never have had a paper existence. This has an impact on its form. The paragraphs are designed to be read on a screen which simultaneously carries other information, and by people thinking about several things at once. They are, for instance, considerably shorter than those usually thought appropriate to academic essays. This illustrates an important general principle. The form of a piece of writing – from an information screen to an academic essay, from a newspaper headline to a company's annual report – is dictated by the use to which it is put. Except for lucidity, there are very few universal stylistic rules.

Version 1 – unedited

LAGERSTEIN CHANGE IN FOUNDATION APPROVED BY MINISTRY OF JUSTICE Pilsville, May 11 (Anglia) – Lagerstein Ltd., the world's 11th-largest brewer, said an application to change the statutes of its foundation was approved by Civilretsdirektoratet, an office under the Ministry of Justice.

Before the amendment the Lagerstein foundation had to control Lagerstein thereby limiting its ability to sell new shares to fund acquisitions.

According to the new statute the foundation will only need control of the parent company, whereas company acquisitions can be paid by stock emissions in the subsidiaries in three different business areas.

The company already started the process of dividing into three business areas before the decision by the Ministry of Justice: Lagerstein Beer, Lagerstein Soft Drink and Lagerstein Finans.

Lagerstein, which sells almost 90 percent of its beer abroad, has been in danger of losing competitiveness because the shareholder by-law dating to 1876 was blocking its expansion plans. Last month, Lagerstein said it was reviewing the finances of Stoutporter Plc's brewing business. The change in the statute will make it easier for Lagerstein to fund such an acquisition even though it may face tough competition from other European brewers.

Version 2 – edited

LAGERSTEIN WINS APPROVAL TO CHANGE THE WAY IT IS CONTROLLED. Pilsville, May 11 (Anglia) – Lagerstein Ltd said the Ministry of Justice approved an application by the No. 11 brewer to change the way the company is controlled.

Previously, the Lagerstein foundation – a group of people appointed by the Royal Academy of Sciences and Letters to supervise research projects and the company's charity work – was required to hold a majority of Lagerstein's stock, limiting its ability to sell shares to fund acquisitions.

Now, the foundation will only be required to hold a majority stake in the parent company, allowing three units in the process of being set up to sell new shares.

The company has already started dividing itself into three units, Lagerstein Beer, Lagerstein Soft Drink and Lagerstein Finans.

> Lagerstein, which sells almost 90 percent of its beer abroad, has been losing competitiveness because the shareholder by-law dating to 1876 blocked its expansion plans.
> The change in the statute will make it easier for Lagerstein to fund acquisitions. Last month, the company said it was reviewing the finances of Stoutporter Plc's brewing business even though it may face competition from other European brewers.

ACTIVITY 7:

Read these two versions of the same story and quickly identify the ways in which improvements have been made.

Editing overview

This list brings together some of the main points made in this chapter. You might use it as a checklist.

- Schedule the editing stage of your work as a central part of the writing process; try to create a gap between composition and editing to help gain perspective and objectivity on what you have written.
- Work with others if possible, especially at the beginning. It is far easier to be objective about someone else's work than your own. It is also less stressful. Be conscious of the emotional context of editing, including the fact that it is tiring and sometimes frustrating.
- Be alert to common cues or danger signals which indicate that editing is likely to be needed. These include:
  - sentences that go on for four lines or more
  - repetitious constructions, words or phrases
  - the presence of clichés
  - points where the ideas you are articulating are complicated or extended
  - having to read a sentence or paragraph two or three times to grasp its meaning
  - repeated patterns of faulty punctuation.
- Be aware of your own verbal mannerisms and/or repeated mistakes that are likely to reoccur.
- Keep your verbs active, your sentences short, and your syntax simple.
- Pay particular attention to beginnings and endings – in other words, the first impressions you make, and the potential pointlessness of formulaic conclusions.
- Be conscious of the need to use an appropriate vocabulary accurately. Use a dictionary and thesaurus to check the accuracy of your usage and extend your word stock.

- Think about the content of your work in terms of the following questions. Are the points I make relevant to the question set? Have I provided adequate evidence for them? Are the points linked together successfully? Have I avoided repetitions?
- When reducing your work to meet a word limit, do so in a fairly systematic and planned way. Do not just hack bits off. Remember that usually you don't have to lose an idea, just trim the way you have expressed it.
- Remember that editing gets easier as you get more experienced at doing it, and – as is the inevitable result of good editing – you become a better writer all round.

Opportunities for practice

The following are invented – and sometimes exaggerated – examples of typical problems that beset undergraduate essays requiring editing. You could use them to practise techniques and develop your skills. They do not set problems that have not been addressed already. They will require you to think about issues of detail, organisation and logical structure.

The first (Activity 8) is the beginning of a good essay. It is not weak work and might achieve an overall mark in the sixties. But it does not make a strong beginning. How might it be improved? The subject of the essay is the work of Angela Carter and Graham Greene in the context of developments in the postwar cultural climate in Britain. The second piece (Activity 9) is nowhere near as good. One notable feature is that it contains lots of small errors, and you could practise proof-reading as well as editing skills to ensure proper punctuation, and that the names of authors are spelt correctly, for instance. You only have about a quarter of the essay. The third and fourth tasks (Activities 10 and 11) again present specific tasks often encountered in undergraduate academic writing.

ACTIVITY 8:

Analyse the strengths and weaknesses of this opening paragraph:

> **With reference to Angela Carter's *The Infernal Desire Machines of Dr Hoffman*, and the work of at least one other writer or film-maker studied on the module, discuss the representation of sexuality in the post-war period.**
>
> In the period of the late 1950s and 1960s, the feeling amongst the masses was one of uncertainty and experimentation. For the first time, people were free to express themselves in terms of their beliefs, their attitudes and their sexuality something which had previously been a taboo subject. It was the first time for music such as rock and

roll and the 'intimate dancing' that accompanied it and the advent of great protests – most notably the CND movement and marches against the Vietnam war. Angela Carter was herself a feminist with ideas on sexuality – as were many women of the time mainly as the contraceptive pill became widely available. Graham Greene also shows us his ideas on sexuality as colonial power crumbles for all countries around the world. It was a time of liberation.

ACTIVITY 9:

This is a more difficult exercise. Imagine you are marking an essay by a new student who has come onto a degree course after years away from education. His confidence is low and his writing skills are rusty. He is unpractised in academic writing and needs guidance about how to go about his next piece of work. He accepts that this is not good enough, but asks 'how do I improve?' You need to tell him just how to go about this by identifying six major points for improvement. It will add an extra dimension to this task if you try yourself to write out some simple instructions for him, bearing in mind – in your tone and what you say – that this is an under-confident, inexperienced writer needful of constructive advice but sensitive to failure. This will allow you to practise management of appropriate tone as well as clarity of explanation.

It doesn't much matter that you may not know the material (though you could look up the poems if you wish). Your advice needs to concentrate on helping the writer to *write*, not to know this work better. You should therefore identify the faults that you think need attention most urgently. Read it through and note major points of weakness. There are numerous errors of punctuation, spelling and so forth, and it would help you to get used to catching these because we all make them. But don't be too preoccupied with this. As a marker you would identify these errors on the essay itself but would also try to concentrate on giving advice on the larger editorial issues at stake.

Make a (longish) list of the essay's faults (including its small errors). If working in a group, discuss your findings with a colleague, identify priorities and consider solutions.

You might think about the following, though it is not an exclusive list. The points are given in no particular order, but might guide your thinking as you read through the piece.

- Does the essay consistently address the question? Does the opening establish the nature of the response and the argument the essay will advance? Is this maintained as the writing progresses?
- Are the points and paragraphs successfully linked together? Are the paragraphs efficient in themselves? (You may wish to refer back to Chapter 4 here.)
- Does the essay disperse points made about a particular issue rather than forming them into a concentrated, sustained discussion?
- Are quotations or other pieces of evidence and information relevant and usefully keyed into the essay? (This is not work by a lazy student, remember, but one who has clearly done some reading and accumulated a reasonable amount of information.) Are quotations apt and well-used?
- Are the sentences clear and word choice effective?

Discuss with reference to at least two writers the ways in which country and city are contrastingly represented in the literature of the period 1880–1930.

This was a period of great change for most societys. Writers wanted to write about the changes, particularly about the growing and changing importance of cities, and a new style of writing was necessary to reflect the change, modernism became popular as did imagism for a short period.

I have selected three writers from this period which, in differing ways, contrast city and country in poetry. They are Edward Thomas, T.S. Eliott and T.E. Hulme.

Thomas poem 'The Mill-Water' was written in 1915 before Thomas died in the First World War. It is a rural poem in terms of both imagery and theme and expresses his unhappiness with way the countryside was being ruined, depopulated and emptied of people. According to Smith, it expresses a typically pessimistic view of life. Thomas found consolation from the nature beauty of the countryside and he wrote lyrically about nature and sadly abut man.

Tomas deals with the inevitability of life contrasting it with nature. 'The Mill-Water', written in 1916, pictures a desolate building 'where the nettle reign's'.

He shows that each person's life is insignificant, no matter how modern and advanced, compared with the history and power of nature.

Thomas expresses this point in the poem as

> Pretty to see, by day
> it's sound is naught
> Compared with thought
> And talk and noise of labour and play. (st. 3)

This extract describes how Edward Thomas feels. It is insignificant compared with nature and history even though he is a poet in a modern society.

Thomas wrote this poem in 1915. In the war he served as an artillery officer and was killed in action. Other poems express his feelings about the war, which were often complicated and divided, as in 'This is no petty case of right and wrong' written on Boxing Day 1915 after an argument with his father about whom he wrote 'he made me sick.'.

'The Mill-water' shows a sense of the world emptying wehich could be a result of the war and could be a result of the rural depopulation Thomas observed in his wanderings: 'Only the sound remains/ of the old mill', this captures the mills destruction and the ending of the way of life it represented: 'only the idle foam/ of water falling,/ changelessly calling,/ where once men had a work-place and a home.' is an evocative last verse.

Thomas responded to the changes around him. Another poet of his period was T. S. Elliot a poet who specialised in the urban landscape he seems to have hated. His style can be compared to Hulmes imagist style but is very different from that of Thomas. In eliot's *The WastLand*, there are many urban image as well as rural images, and often they are contrasted. In Hulme's poem 'Autumn' the images are rural although the meaning is an observation of urban poverty, shown in the last line.

Hulmes poem 'Autumn' shows typically how rural and urban images were juxtapositioned by imagists. The poem contrasts; it starts with a description of an Autumn night and the Moon at sunset but concludes with a totally different tone, an image of urban poor town children.

Both the Waste Land and 'Autumn show concern for the state of modern life but the use of contrasting urban and rural images as well. It describes the sunrise as 'saw the ruddy moon lean over the hedge like a red-faced farmer' which is an accurate image of the Moon rising as night falls. 'Autumn' is infact a poem about inner-city poverty and this is the contrast that Hulme' incorporated into 'Autumn'.

Hulme has seen poverty and suffering and is precise about his description like the imagists were. He made a statement, about the changes he observed and Eliot shows his lack of faith in modern society and desolatation, caused by the great war in the *Waste Land* in the title of his poem. This is a biblical reference as Christ dies to save the waste land. Elyot uses this myth to comment upon the state of modern cities and culture and the changes in rural life.

Like Thomas and Hume Elliot, uses strong imagery to describe modern life. This is necessary. Eliot writes of the 'river's tent' being broken and the spoilt vegetation brings home the longing for a more pastoral life which is like Thomas in 'The Mill-River'. He unites the world of the county and the city by emphasising their difference from each other, now.... [*the essay continues*]

ACTIVITY 10:

Here is a common kind of task in English syllabuses: the request for a critical commentary on a particular poem or prose passage. You are no doubt familiar with these from 'A' level, or Access, as well as from degree-level work. Teachers set these sort of tasks because they develop your reading and interpretative skills. But they also offer the opportunity to write briefly and effectively in a format that concentrates your attention on a limited amount of material. What is being tested alongside your reading skills is the ability to convey your ideas clearly, succinctly, accurately and efficiently, using appropriate vocabulary (including technical terms where appropriate).

Usually, such exercises are short (maybe as little as 500 words) and the question frequently directs you to a particular topic for consideration. Markers therefore expect a clear focus in the answer, an attention to textual detail from the passage or poem given, and succinct and clear writing which makes the most of the limited space available to you. It is important to recognise that these are general writing skills appropriate to *all* academic writing. Here is the question:

Discuss the way Hardy's poem 'The Man He Killed' creates a sense of character by using the dramatic monologue form*.

[* A 'dramatic monologue' is a poem which is spoken by a character as if in a play. The poet's intention is to create a character who speaks in his/her own 'voice' by using language which is appropriate to the character's life in terms of, for example, social class or occupation or region or period or gender, but which is also revealing of the speaker's particular personality and experiences.]

'The Man He Killed'

'Had he and I but met
By some old ancient inn,
We should have sat us down to wet
Right many a nipperkin!

'But ranged as infantry,   5
And staring face to face,
I shot at him as he at me,
And killed him in his place.

'I shot him dead because –
Because he was my foe,   10
Just so: my foe of course he was:
That's clear enough; although

'He thought he'd list, perhaps,
Off-hand like – just as I –
Was out of work – had sold his traps –   15
No other reason why.

'Yes; quaint and curious war is!
You shoot a fellow down
You'd treat if met where any bar is,
Or help to half-a-crown.'   20

(Hardy 1976: 287)

The answer you will find below has been invented for the purposes of this exercise. It is fairly accurate as far as textual and contextual details are concerned, but it is not a particularly distinguished piece of writing. It is reasonably technically competent, but is too long and not very effective in relation to the task set. It is organisationally messy; it doesn't always stick to the topic; and it confuses general knowledge with critical analysis. It also contains examples of poor sentence construction and logical flaws. (For example, look at the beginning of the fourth sentence: 'Though a life-long poet, his novels are frequently tragic . . .'. There is, of course, no necessary connection between being a poet and not writing tragically.)

In short, this piece badly needs editing. It demonstrates a grasp of some information (some of it not relevant), contains some useful interpretative points, and there is enough here to make a good answer. How might we achieve this? This is your task.

First read through both the poem and the critical response to it, making any notes you feel are appropriate. Then work in pairs to produce a better version of the commentary, discussing the points as you go through them. You may find this list of questions helpful.

- Is the first paragraph a clear response to the question and a good introduction to the ideas the piece will present overall?
- In the body of the answer, what would you leave out?
- What points would you develop? (You may not have time to do this now in detail, but you should indicate where you think development may be helpful. For instance, do you think any further detail or evidence might be useful?)
- Do any individual sentences need editing to make them more pointed or effective?
- Are the expressions chosen appropriate and accurately used?
- Does the piece overall construct a sequential, orderly argument? Might you rearrange part of it (for instance, the order of the paragraphs)?
- Are there any logical flaws of the kind mentioned above?
- Does the piece end well?

You will need to make decisions about what material is important and what is not. This may involve a complex dismantling of individual sentences or paragraphs. The finished version should be no longer than 650 words.

Thomas Hardy (1840–1928) was born in Dorset, where he lived much of his life, training as an architect before making his name with a series of novels begun in the late 1860s. Many of these, like *Tess of the d'Urbervilles* and *Jude the Obscure*, are now classics, and some of their themes are evident in this poem. In particular, Hardy was a pessimist. Though a life-long poet, his novels are frequently tragic, and centre on the unfortunate consequences of everyday incidents among ordinary people whose lives are ruined or spoilt by unhappy acts, or choices, or love affairs. The gloomy outlook of this poem seems to be of this kind. It features an ordinary man caught in a situation he can neither control nor properly understand. The poem describes his attempt to rationalise the fact that he has killed a man in wartime and his attempts to come to terms with something he would not have done had he been living in the ordinary pattern of his life at home in Dorset (we assume) undertaking his usual occupation and living among his family, neighbours and friends and going about his daily business in an accustomed way that has been passed down through the generations before the catastrophe that has caused his present bewilderment.

The plight of the common soldier in war is a common theme in literature, and writers such as Wilfred Owen, or even Shakespeare, explore it, though very few of them look at the situation from the point of view of the common soldier, preferring instead the perspective of the officer or civilian. Though Hardy never fought in a war himself, he often wrote about it, or about soldiers (like Sergeant Troy in *Far From the Madding Crowd*), and he manages in this poem to achieve this, entering the mind of an ordinary man whose experiences he recreates. The poem is a dramatic monologue, though it is very moving and achieves the purposes Hardy designed for it, which is to make the reader feel sympathy for the speaker and be aware of his predicament.

The dramatic monologue is a poem which is spoken by a character as if in a play. The poet's intention is to create a character who speaks in his/her own 'voice' by using language which is appropriate to the character's life but which is also revealing of the speaker's particular personality and experiences. In this poem the language is appropriate to the kind of person who speaks it, who is a sort of craftsman or tradesman who has been down on his luck and on his uppers and speaks a colloquial language appropriate to this kind of person. Despite this, the poem is not irrational or absurd, and it is clear and easily understandable, though some words are obscure and seem to be put there for local colour or light relief. There are few metaphors or images or symbols and the poem does not use poetic devices. Craftsmen often have restricted language. The rhythm of the poem is very smooth for most of the time and it rhymes ABAB like a ballad. In the third and fourth stanzas, though, the syntax is more complicated and difficult to understand. Why?

This could be because it is at this point that the speaker is most puzzled by his actions. He repeats himself, pauses and hesitates. He falters and fluctuates, as though he were asking himself questions which he can't answer, and so he moves on to repeating the things he had been told by officers or patriotic people or both: 'He was my foe,/Just so: my foe of course he was:/That's clear enough;'. The 'although' after this creates a hesitation by being placed in the middle of the poem at the end of a line and at the end of a stanza. There are other examples of this technique in the poem.

The conclusion to the poem is odd as the speaker dismisses his thoughts with a shrug. The personal 'he' becomes the anonymous and abstract 'fellow', and it is as if the questions he has been asking himself in the subconscious of his mind are now being denied: 'no other reason why'. 'Quaint and curious' are inappropriate words for death and war, as though the man is not clever enough to see his actions as they really are: 'you shoot a fellow down' avoids saying that he killed him. We all cover up actions we feel guilty about in our lives. These words go back to the beginning of the poem and especially 'old ancient' which seems to say the same thing twice but creates the simplicity of the character and may suggest that it is being pushed back into the past by the speaker and give an image of what is being fought for in the war. The old rural countryside.

The first verse sets the scene of ordinary life in 'some old ancient inn' where he is having a drink, or might be, with the man he has killed if he had not killed him before. The mood is relaxed – or so he imagines – the scene is recognisable and a bit charming to us, though it is maybe a bit sentimental (which is unfortunate) and 'country-cottage' or 'heritage-like'. 'Nipperkin' is not a familiar word, but its meaning is obvious from the context. It means drink. This appears a happy place, though later there is unemployment. It creates a rather 'country-yokel' atmosphere full of thatched cottages and green wellies.

The second paragraph is a war scene in which the speaker is shot at by the man he killed as he shot at him so there is no question of this being a cold-blooded murder or crime. 'Ranged' suggests not only that they were spread out in a line, but also because we use the word range in relation to guns as in 'he is in range. Fire!' The rhythm is still gentle and peaceful and the verse rhymes ABAB like the first. Though this one is destructive, as wars are.

Finally, though the poem confronts a potentially tragic fate it manages to gain a more optimistic outlook on a dreadful situation by the close. [about 1025 words]

ACTIVITY 12:

This exercise is designed to develop your ability to take an over-complicated sentence and edit it into something clear and readable. The sentence in question might be characterised as the one with the over-used semi-colon, several 'buts' and straggly logic. It is a common breed found in all walks of life. The aim of the exercise is to improve the sentence, which summarises some of the ideas of Adrienne Rich. You may re-arrange it, divide it into several different sentences, re-punctuate it or add to it. But you should *not* change its overall meaning. If you are working in a group it would be helpful to work on this on your own at first, and then exchange ideas with a neighbour to produce a finished version.

The fact that the child needs a mother is not disputed; but Rich does attack the 'cast' that society puts on women to be mothers, a woman cannot be seen as having her own identity without possessing the potential role of mother; Rich says women can be good mothers but they can also be just women, the two can work together.

The sentence contains the following propositions:

- children need mothers
- Rich attacks the way women are 'cast' in their role as mothers
- this 'casting' excludes a woman's individuality
- her social identity depends upon her potential to be a mother
- motherhood and personal identity can work together.

Summary

In this chapter we have looked at a number of key editing skills including:

- editing openings
- word choice
- techniques for ensuring clarity and fluency of expression
- techniques for ensuring concision
- editing in the real world

- editing endings
- cutting back to the word limit.

References

Blake, William (1979) *Blake's Poetry and Designs*, ed. Mary Lynn Johnson and John E. Grant. London: Norton.

Davies, Norman (1997) *Europe: A History*. London: Pimlico.

Hardy, Thomas (1976) *The Complete Poems*. London: Macmillan.

Rylance, Rick (2000) 'Twisting: Memory from Eliot to Eliot' in Sally Shuttleworth, Jaqueline Labbe and Matthew Campbell (eds), *Memory and Memorials 1789–1914*. London: Routledge.

Weldon, Fay (1983) *The Life and Loves of a She-Devil*. London: Hodder and Stoughton.

References and bibliographies

Anna Snaith

Accurate and consistent referencing is an essential part of the essay writing process. This is so that readers of your work can track down the sources from which you quote or to which you refer. These sources may be books, newspaper articles or web sites: this chapter will give details on how to reference numerous types of sources. Referencing is also important so as to avoid plagiarism, or passing off other people's work as your own.

Acknowledging others' ideas through references ensures that no one can accuse you of plagiarism. Writing and research is all about building on the work of other critics and writers, so it is highly likely that you will make reference to primary or secondary sources, or both, but make sure you acknowledge them. As you work, take full and accurate notes about the books you are consulting and the page numbers from which you take quotations. This will make your life easier when you come to compile a bibliography.

This chapter will explain and give examples of three of the most commonly used referencing and bibliographic styles in the humanities (but note that publishers often have their own house style, as you will see from this book). These styles are called the MLA (Modern Languages Association) system, the APA (American Psychological Association) system and the MHRA (Modern Humanities Research Association) system. If you are producing essays for a particular institution, make sure you find out what their preferred system is. They may specify that you should use one of these three styles, or they may use another system.

The MLA and APA systems are both parenthetical: that is, bracketed references in the body of your essay are linked to full citations in your bibliography. This eliminates the need for notes. The MHRA system, in contrast, uses notes instead of bracketed references: that is, superscript note numbers in your essay are linked to a sequence of notes which appear either at the foot of the page or in a section at the end of your essay. More and more, writers and researchers in the humanities are favouring parenthetical styles because readers do not have to keep referring to the notes to find out the source of a quotation or a reference.

You will need to make sure that you present and punctuate your references consistently. If you are using the APA system, for example, you might choose to write a text reference as (Smith 1990: 25–6) or (Smith, 1990, pp. 25–6), but use the same style for all references in an essay. The examples in this chapter demonstrate some common styles of punctuation in references and you could follow these.

The MLA system

Text references

With the MLA system the bracket in the body of the essay contains only the author's last name and a page number: (Jones 36). Note that there is no date, as there is with the APA system. The purpose of the bracketed reference is to give the page number and to allow the reader to link it to a full citation in the bibliography. Here's an example of what the reference looks like in your essay:

> This point has recently been argued at some length (Khan 35–7).

With most sources this should be straightforward, but there are a few more complicated situations.

- Two or more authors
  If a book has two authors, the citation should include both names: (Jones and Barnardo 25). If there are more than three authors use the abbreviation 'et al.': (Lightfoot et al. 342–5). Note that 'et al.' needs a full stop because it is an abbreviation for 'et alii'.
- Two authors with the same name
  In this case, use the first initial to distinguish the references: (L. Bolden 47).
- Two works by the same author
  Here, you will need to use a shortened version of the title to distinguish the sources: (Rushdie, *Homelands* 55).
- Plays and poems
  When referring to classic verse plays or poems, omit the page number altogether and instead cite the act, scene and line numbers for a play or

just the line numbers for a poem. This means that readers with any edition of the play or poem can find the reference. You can use arabic or roman numerals for plays: (*Hamlet* II.ii.21–5) or (*Hamlet* 2.2.21–5). Abbreviate titles of plays or poems: e.g. ('Autumn' 11–14) for Keats's 'Ode to Autumn'.

One important rule of thumb for parenthetical references in the text in both APA and MLA styles is only to include what is necessary. If, for example, in your sentence you have already named the author, then you can omit his or her name from the reference:

Khan argues this point at some length (35–7).

If you cite two quotations from the same text in quick succession, and it is obvious to the reader that they are taken from the same source, then you do not need to repeat the author's name in the second reference. The main points to remember are clarity and brevity. Do not add unnecessary references: make things easy for the reader rather than cluttering up your writing with references.

Bibliography (or Works Cited)

The bibliography is a list at the end of your essay which includes all the sources from which you have quoted or to which you have referred. This list provides the full citation for the sources which you cited briefly in the bracketed references in the body of the essay. Order the items alphabetically by the author's last name. Several books by the same author should be ordered chronologically, but after the first entry, omit the author's name and put a long dash in its place. The first line of each reference should be flush with the margin and subsequent lines should be indented. Italicise (or underline) all titles.

A basic entry should include, in this order: the author's name, the title of the book, the place of publication, the publisher, and the date. For example:

Barker, Pat. *Regeneration*. London: Penguin, 1992.

Now we will look at some more complex kinds of entry.

- Two or more authors

Kerrigan, William, and Gordon Braden. *The Idea of the Renaissance*. Baltimore: Johns Hopkins University Press, 1989.

The authors are listed in the order in which they appear on the title page. If there are three authors or more, you can name the first one and then add 'et al.'.

- Editor(s) as author

> Frye, Northrop, ed. *Sound and Poetry*. New York: Columbia University Press, 1957.
> Lenz, C.R.S., G. Greene and C.T. Neely, eds. *The Woman's Part: Feminist Criticism of Shakespeare*. Champaign: University of Illinois Press, 1980.

- Author and editor(s) or translator(s)

> Pound, Ezra. *Literary Essays*. Ed. T.S. Eliot. New York: New Directions, 1953.
> Ariès, P. *Centuries of Childhood: A Social History of Family Life*. Trans. R. Baldock. New York: Knopf, 1962.

The name of the editor or translator goes immediately after the title. Here 'ed.' means 'edited by' rather than 'editor', so the abbreviation should still be 'ed.' for more than one editor.

- Quoting from the Introduction to a primary text

> Drabble, Margaret. Introduction. *Middlemarch*. By George Eliot. New York: Bantam, 1982. v–xi.

This is the entry style if you have actually quoted from or referred to the introduction itself. The bracketed citation in your essay would look like this: (Drabble xi). In general, if you quote from part of a book (an introduction or a chapter) which has a different author from the rest or other parts of the book, you cite the author of the particular part from which you quoted. Because you have cited the author of that particular part, that author's name must begin your bibliographic entry so that the reader can match up the entries.

- Specific chapters in a book

> Greenblatt, Stephen. 'Invisible Bullets: Renaissance Authority and its Subversion, *Henry IV* and *Henry V*.' In *Political Shakespeare: Essays in Cultural Materialism*. Ed. Jonathan Dollimore and Alan Sinfield. Manchester: Manchester University Press, 1994. 18–47.

Here, the entry includes the inclusive page numbers of the chapter.

- Subsequent editions

> Crystal, David. *Rediscover Grammar*. 2nd edn. Harlow: Longman, 1996.

- Modern editions of a primary text

> Gissing, George. *New Grub Street*. 1891. Ed. Bernard Bergonzi. London: Penguin, 1985.

The initial date of publication is placed after the title, and the date of the modern edition goes in the usual place at the end of the entry.

- Multi-volume works

> Woolf, Virginia. *The Diary of Virginia Woolf*. Ed. A.O. Bell. 5 vols. London: The Hogarth Press, 1978–84.

Make sure you include the dates of publication of all the volumes, as shown. If you are citing only one volume, substitute 'Vol. 1', say, for '5 vols', and give just the date of that volume.

- Journal articles

> Albright, Daniel. 'Virginia Woolf As Autobiographer.' *The Kenyon Review* 6.4 (1984): 1–17.

- Newspaper articles

> Rosser, Susan. 'Scientists Discover Literacy Gene.' *New York Times* 22 Mar. 1994, late edn: A1.

If the newspaper has several daily editions, cite the edition after the date.

- Films

> *Like Water for Chocolate*. Dir. Alfonso Arau. Miramax, 1993.

You can start with the director, an actor, or the writer, if you are citing that particular person's contribution (e.g. Arau, Alfonso, dir.). The basic information needed is title, director, distributor and date, but other information can be included if relevant to your use of the film in your essay.

- CD-ROMs and portable databases
  More and more information and textual sources are now available in electronic format, on the internet, on CD-ROM or other forms of portable database. Since this is a recent development many style manuals do not include information on how to cite electronic sources. Let us start with CD-ROMs and other portable databases. These are similar to books in that they are created by publishers, they come in editions, and they are a product that can be bought (as distinct from online sources). There are some differences, however, which affect the citation procedure. You need to cite: the publication medium, such as CD-ROM, diskette or magnetic tape, because the material might appear differently in different formats; the vendor's name, because the vendor is often different from the organisation which compiled the information (there may be several vendors of

a particular database, therefore the material could be presented differently – the vendor's name is usually found on the title screen); and the date of electronic publication, because some databases are updated regularly. You may also need to include two dates: the original date of publication of, say, a newspaper article or a literary text, and the date of electronic release. The latter date is usually found on the title screen.

> Angier, Natalie. 'Chemists Learn Why Vegetables Are Good For You.' *New York Times* 13 Apr. 1993. *New York Times Ondisc.* CD-ROM. Oct. 1993.

- Online material

> Alston, Robin. 'The Battle of the Books.' *Humanist* 7.0176 (10 Sept. 1993): 10 pp. Online. Internet. 10 Oct. 1993.

The material is cited like a journal article. Include the word 'Online' and the name of the computer network (e.g. 'Internet') and then the date of retrieval.

The APA system

Text references

With the APA (or author–date) system the bracketed references in the body of your essay contain the author's name, the date of publication of the text, and the page number: (Jones, 1995, p. 36). This reference allows the reader to find the fuller reference which will appear in the bibliography under Jones. It is important that the name and date given in the text correlate precisely with the entry in the bibliography. Here's an example of what the reference looks like in your essay:

> This point has recently been argued at some length (Khan, 1990, pp. 35–7).

Notice that the bracketed citation goes at the end of the sentence before the full stop. Even if your quotation appears at or near the beginning of your sentence, you should still put the citation right before the full stop. This is so that it interrupts the reader's flow as little as possible.

- Two or more authors
  If a book has two authors, the citation should include both names: (Khan and Schuster, 1992, p. 47). If a book has three or more authors, use the abbreviation 'et al.': (King et al., 1997, pp. 68–73).

- Two works by one author published in the same year
  If you are quoting from two or more works by one author with the same publication date, then you need to add lower case letters to the date. This needs to be done in the bibliography as well. For example: (Price, 1998a, pp. 35–6) and (Price, 1998b, p. 46).

Bibliography

The list is made in alphabetical order of the authors' last names. All works written by the same author should appear in chronological order. The entry for a book with several authors should list all the authors (not using et al. as in the text citation) and they should appear in the order that they appear on the title page of the book. Italicise (or underline) all book titles.

A basic entry includes, in this order: the author's name, the date of publication, the title of the book, the place of publication, and the publisher. For example:

> Barker, P. (1992). *Regeneration*. London: Penguin.

Here, we can see why this system is called the author–date system: because the date follows immediately after the author's name, whereas in other systems the date goes at the end of the entry.

This is the simplest kind of entry that you will need. Now we will look at more complicated kinds of entries. Don't be intimidated by the variety of types of entry. They are actually easy to understand and the conventions are logical.

- Two or more authors

> Kerrigan, W., and Braden, G. (1989). *The Idea of the Renaissance*. Baltimore: Johns Hopkins University Press.

- Editor(s) as author

> Frye, N. (ed.). (1957). *Sound and Poetry*. New York: Columbia University Press.
> Lenz, C.R.S., Greene, G., and Neely, C.T. (eds). (1980). *The Woman's Part: Feminist Criticism of Shakespeare*. Champaign: University of Illinois Press.

- Author and editor(s) or translator(s)

> Pound, E. (1953). *Literary Essays*. Ed. T.S. Eliot. New York: New Directions.
> Ariès, P. (1962). *Centuries of Childhood: A Social History of Family Life*. Trans. R. Baldock. New York: Knopf.

- Quoting from the Introduction to a primary text

  > Drabble, M. (1982). Introduction to *Middlemarch* by George Eliot. New York: Bantam.

- Specific chapters in a book

  > Greenblatt, S. (1994). Invisible Bullets: Renaissance Authority and its Subversion, *Henry IV* and *Henry V*. In J. Dollimore and A. Sinfield (eds), *Political Shakespeare: Essays in Cultural Materialism*. Manchester: Manchester University Press. 18–47.

- Subsequent editions

  > Crystal, D. (1996). *Rediscover Grammar*. (2nd edn). Harlow: Longman.

- Modern editions of a primary text

  > Gissing, G. (1985). *New Grub Street*. (1891). Ed. Bernard Bergonzi. London: Penguin.

The first date cited is the date of the modern edition, and the original date of publication is cited in brackets immediately after the title.

- Multi-volume works

  > Woolf, V. (1978–84). *The Diary of Virginia Woolf*. (Vols 1–5). Ed. A.O. Bell. London: The Hogarth Press.

- Citing one particular volume

  > Woolf, V. (1984). *The Diary of Virginia Woolf*. (Vol. 5). Ed. A.O. Bell. London: The Hogarth Press.

- Journal articles

  > Albright, D. (1984). Virginia Woolf As Autobiographer. *The Kenyon Review* 6 (4): 1–17.

- Newspaper articles

  > Rosser, S. (1994, 22 March). 'Scientists Discover Literacy Gene.' *New York Times*, late edn: A1.

When a periodical such as a newspaper has a monthly or daily date of publication, this is included in the date bracket after the author's name.

- Films

> Arau, A. (1993). *Like Water for Chocolate*. Miramax.

- CD-ROMs and portable databases

> Angier, N. (1993, 13 April). Chemists learn why vegetables are good for you. *New York Times*. *New York Times Ondisc*. CD-ROM. Oct. 1993.

Here the newspaper article is cited in the conventional manner, and then the database information is provided: the name of the database, the medium (CD-ROM) and the date of electronic publication.

- Online material

> Kenneth, I. (1995). A Buddhist response to the nature of human rights. [9 pars.] *Journal of Buddhist Ethics* [online serial], 2. Available: http://www.cac.psu.edu/jbe/twocont.html. (15 June 1998).
> Daly, B. (1970). *Writing Argumentative Essays* [online]. Available: http://cougar.vut.edu.au/dalbj/argueweb/frntpage.htm. (12 May 1998).

Include the web address for World Wide Web sites.

> Using American Psychological Association (APA) format. (1998). *Purdue OWL handouts* [online]. Available: http://owl.english.purdue.edu/Files/34.html. (9 September 1998).

Often there will not be an author for a website, in which case start your reference with the title of the web page. NB: You may actually want to consult the above web page when you are compiling your bibliographies.

- E-mail
  E-mail is a personal communication, therefore you do not need to include it in your bibliography. If you quote from e-mail correspondence, you only need a parenthetical citation in the body of your essay: e.g. (Andrea Brown, e-mail to author, 9 September 1998).

The MHRA system

With this system, full citations in the form of notes eliminate the need for a bibliography. A basic note includes: the author's name, the title of the book, the place of publication, the publisher, and the date. Here's an example of a note reference:

> 1. Pat Barker, *Regeneration* (London: Penguin, 1992), p. 45.

Below are the conventions for various types of sources. Importantly, this is for the first citation. If you cite the source a second time, an abbreviated form is enough. See below for further details.

- Two or more authors

  1. William Kerrigan and Gordon Braden, *The Idea of the Renaissance* (Baltimore: Johns Hopkins University Press, 1989), pp. 34–5.

- Editor(s) as author

  1. Northrop Frye (ed.), *Sound and Poetry* (New York: Columbia University Press, 1957); C.R.S. Lenz, G. Greene and C.T. Neely (eds), *The Woman's Part: Feminist Criticism of Shakespeare* (Champaign: University of Illinois Press, 1980).

- Author and editor(s) or translator(s)

  1. Ezra Pound, *Literary Essays*, ed. T.S. Eliot (New York: New Directions, 1953); P. Ariès, *Centuries of Childhood: A Social History of Family Life*, trans. R. Baldock (New York: Knopf, 1962).

- Quoting from the Introduction to a primary text

  1. Margaret Drabble, 'Introduction', in *Middlemarch*, by George Eliot (New York: Bantam, 1982), pp. v–xi.

- Specific chapters in a book

  1. Stephen Greenblatt, 'Invisible Bullets: Renaissance Authority and its Subversion, *Henry IV* and *Henry V*', in *Political Shakespeare: Essays in Cultural Materialism*, ed. Jonathan Dollimore and Alan Sinfield (Manchester: Manchester University Press, 1994), pp. 18–47 (p. 41).

After the publication details, include the page numbers of the whole article, and then the page number from which you have quoted in brackets.

- Subsequent editions

  1. David Crystal, *Rediscover Grammar*, 2nd edn (Harlow: Longman, 1996).

- Modern editions of a primary text

  1. George Gissing, *New Grub Street* (1891), ed. Bernard Bergonzi (London: Penguin, 1985).

- Multi-volume works

  > 1. Virginia Woolf, *The Diary of Virginia Woolf*, ed. A.O. Bell, 5 vols (London: The Hogarth Press, 1978–84).

- Journal articles

  > 1. Daniel Albright, 'Virginia Woolf As Autobiographer', *The Kenyon Review*, 6.4 (1984), 1–17 (16).

Again, if you are referring to a specific page, cite that in brackets after the full page reference.

- Newspaper articles

  > 1. Susan Rosser, 'Scientists Discover Literacy Gene', *New York Times*, 22 March 1994, late edn, p. A1.

- Films

  > 1. *Like Water for Chocolate*, dir. A. Arau, Miramax, 1993.

Subsequent references

Give a full reference for each work in the first instance; thereafter use the shortest form possible. Usually this will be: 'Smith, p. 62.' If there is ambiguity, for example you have cited two texts by the same author, then include an abbreviated version of the title: 'Smith, *On Hamlet*, p. 62'.

Quotations

When writing your essays, you will inevitably want to quote from other texts: either from primary texts or from secondary works of criticism. You need to use quotations to back up your arguments. You should avoid, however, the overuse of quotation. Substantiate your own ideas with judiciously chosen quotations, rather than writing an essay which is merely a list of quotations strung together. You may lose marks if quotations are presented incorrectly, or if you have misquoted your source text. As you are working and reading, keep full and accurate notes of quotations and where they come from.

Now we will look at how to present quotations in your essays. There are three different ways of quoting within your writing:

- you can work the direct quotation into your own sentences
- you can include an extensive quotation by using an indented paragraph
- you can summarise or paraphrase the quotation in your own words.

Quotation worked into your own prose

Use single quotation marks ('. . .'), except for quotations within quotations, where double quotation marks should be used ('. . . ". . ." . . .'). Punctuation marks immediately before a quotation depend on its syntactical relationship to what precedes it. No punctuation, or at most a comma, is required if the quotation makes your own sentence grammatically complete. For example:

> Moll Flanders describes the inmates of Newgate Prison as 'a crew of hellhounds' (Defoe, 1978, p. 262).

> The inmates of Newgate were, according to Moll, 'a crew of hellhounds' (Defoe, 1978, p. 262).

But obviously if you are quoting often from the same primary text, then after the first full reference, as above, you need only supply the page number in brackets after subsequent quotations. Your bibliography provides further details of the edition you are using.

A colon is needed if your introductory statement is grammatically complete in itself. For example:

> Moll makes a rare venture into figurative language to describe the conditioning effect of Newgate: 'Like the water in the hollows of mountains, which petrifies and turns into stone whatever they are suffered to drop upon, so the continual conversing with such a crew of hellhounds had the same common operation upon me as upon other people' (p. 262).

Extensive quotations separated from your own prose

Prose quotation of more than sixty words and verse quotation of more than one line should be separated from your commentary, set off by a colon, and indented. Do not use quotation marks with indented quotations: the indent signals that this is a quotation. But lengthy quotation should be used very sparingly; a particular point is unlikely to be clearly and crisply illustrated by just quoting a lot. If you do quote at length, make sure the commentary you make on the quotation justifies the length.

In indented verse quotations be careful to preserve the metrical form, punctuation, stanza forms and line endings. Supply line numbers in parenthesis after verse quotation. For example:

> Let us go then, you and I,
> When the evening is spread out against the sky
> Like a patient etherised upon a table;
> (T.S. Eliot, 'The Love Song of J. Alfred Prufrock', ll. 1–3)

Quotations from plays divided into acts and scenes should supply act, scene and line numbers. Some critics use upper-case roman numerals for acts, lower-case roman numerals for scenes, and ordinary numerals for line numbers. For example:

> There's language in her eye, her cheek, her lip;
> (*Troilus and Cressida* IV.vi.56).

But ordinary numerals for act, scene and line number, separated by a full stop, can be less confusing: *Troilus and Cressida* 4.6.56.

Summary or paraphrase in your own words

If you are using someone else's ideas, but summarising or paraphrasing them in your own words, remember to attribute them accordingly: include the bracketed reference after your summary or paraphrase. For example:

> One well known critical account of *Moll Flanders* denies that it is an intentionally ironic work (Watt, 1957, p. 135).

REMEMBER: unacknowledged use of other people's ideas is plagiarism (see above).

Standard abbreviations

Here are a few of the standard abbreviations used in literary essays and references:

ed.	edited by, or editor
edn	edition
cf.	compare
sic	thus in the source (i.e. if there's a mistake in the source you're quoting)
l.	line (of poetry)
ll.	lines
p.	page
pp.	pages
rpt	reprint
trans.	translator, translated by, translation
vol.	volume
CD-ROM	compact disc read-only memory
et al.	and others: 'al.' is short for 'alii', and so needs a full stop.

ACTIVITY 1:

Make a bibliography out of the following information, first in APA style, and then in MLA style:

- A book called The Romantic Poets by Marianne Shaw published in 1997 by Macmillan in Basingstoke.
- A book called The Garden Party by Ann Shelley originally published in 1876 and republished by Oxford University Press, in Oxford, in 1992 and edited by Grace McDermot.
- A journal article called 'Re-visioning Audience in the Late Works of Walter Browbridge' by Steve Hedges published in a journal called Text in 1988 in volume 3 number 5 on pages 66–88.
- An essay called 'Looking Backward: The Role of History in the Work of Lucy Mowbray' by Catherine Lowell in a book of essays called Women Writers edited by Carol Jones published by Cambridge University Press in Cambridge in 1990.
- A book called Der Freund by Hans Gottlieb originally published in 1912 translated by Michael Zorn in 1956 and published by Penguin in Harmondsworth.

ACTIVITY 2:

Choose a particular topic that interests you and go to the library and make a ten-item bibliography of sources relevant to that topic. Try to include different types of sources in the bibliography: books, articles, websites etc.

ACTIVITY 3:

Go back to an essay which you have written and check your use of references and bibliography. Can you find any mistakes in your work? What corrections need to be made?

ACTIVITY 4:

Look on the web for sites on a topic of your choice. Make a bibliography of those sites using either the APA or MLA systems.

Appendix

'Composition, Distribution, Arrangement: Form and Structure in Jane Austen's Novels' from *After Bakhtin: Essays on Fiction and Criticism* (David Lodge, 1990), London: Routledge

E ach of Jane Austen's novels has its own distinctive identity, but they also have a strong family resemblance, one to another. What kind of fiction did she write, and what was special about it? The short answer is that she fused together the sentimental novel and the comedy of manners with an unprecedented effect of realism. A longer answer will entail a description of these categories and qualities in terms of narrative form and structure.

By the 'sentimental novel', in this context, I mean the didactic, heroine-centred love story of which the prototype was Samuel Richardson's *Pamela; or Virtue Rewarded* (1740–1) and which survives today in the popular women's fiction generally known as 'romance'. This latter designation is some-what ironic since Samuel Richardson prided himself on writing a kind of prose fiction that eschewed the characteristic devices and implausibilities of traditional romance and would be morally improving precisely because it was 'true to life'. The eponymous heroine of *Pamela* is a young maidservant in a great house who, at the death of her mistress, is subjected to the sexual advances of the latter's son and heir, Mr B——. Although she admires her master, the principled Pamela resists all his efforts to seduce her with such spirit and steadfastness that his lust is converted into love and he eventually makes her his wife. The story, which Richardson claimed was based on an actual case, is told entirely in the form of letters and journal entries, mostly written by the heroine; and it initiated a long line of sentimental epistolary novels, among them the first version of *Sense and Sensibility*, called *Elinor and Marianne*. Richardson's epistolary technique became obsolete with the development (in which Jane Austen played a crucial part) of more subtle and flexible methods of representing a character's thoughts and feelings in literary narrative. The basic structure of *Pamela* as a love story has, however, had a remarkably long life and proved adaptable to many literary purposes, high and low. Though invented by a male author, it is an essentially feminine kind of fiction, usually written by women, centred on a heroine rather than a hero, and directed particularly at a female audience. It arose at a time when women were beginning to assert their right to choose their partners in marriage but were restricted by social convention to a very passive role in the courtship process. The 'happy ending' of the didactic love story rewards the heroine, who copes with various emotional, social, economic and ethical obstacles to union with the man she loves without losing her integrity. If there were no obstacles, of course, there would be no story.

Structurally, then, the love story consists of the delayed fulfilment of a desire. The delay puts the heroine under stress and thus generates the 'sentiment' – that is, the representation of feelings, anxieties and moral choices that is the real source of interest and value in the sentimental novel. In *Pamela*, the cause of delay is very simple: Mr B—— wants extramarital sex, but Pamela wants love and marriage, and eventually she wins. This plot was too explicitly sexual, and perhaps too democratic in its implications (Pamela is promoted from the bottom to the top of the class system by sticking to her principles), for Richardson's more genteel, mainly female successors in the sentimental novel tradition, such as Fanny Burney, Maria Edgeworth and Jane Austen. The heroine, though often inferior to the hero in social status and fortune, is not as remote in class terms as Pamela was from Mr B—— before her marriage. The hero is not morally compromised by having designs on the heroine's purity, and illicit sexuality is displaced on to other characters – a seducer whose designs are frustrated by the hero, for instance, or a seductress or 'fallen woman' who throws into relief the heroine's moral integrity. The necessary delay in the union of hero and heroine then has to be contrived by other means. For example, the lovers get off on the wrong foot, and one or both take some time to recognize the true nature of their feelings; they are alienated by misunderstandings, by other characters' intrigues, by apparently insurmountable obstacles to do with fortune, family prejudice and the like. In many of these novels (e.g. Fanny Burney's *Evelina* [1778] and Maria Edgeworth's *Belinda* [1801]), some of the romance motifs that Richardson had rigorously excluded from his *Pamela* begin to seep back into the sentimental novel as a way of resolving the plot in a flurry of wills, confessions, discoveries of long-lost daughters/sons/parents and so on. Jane Austen did not use such devices; indeed, she pointedly abstained from them. But all her novels have the basic structure of the didactic love story that derived from Richardson, albeit with much variation, modification, displacement and even inversion of its basic components.

Of all Jane Austen's works, perhaps *Pride and Prejudice* cleaves most closely to the paradigm of the classic love story. Here the delay of the lover's union is caused by their mutually unfavourable 'first impressions' (the original title of the novel). Darcy offends Elizabeth by his arrogance, by his interference in the promising relationship between Mr Bingley and her sister Jane, and by his alleged ill-treatment of Wickham. She refuses his first, totally unexpected proposal of marriage, thus demonstrating her integrity as well as her impulsiveness, because the match is a tempting one in material terms. When, for a number of reasons, her feelings toward Darcy change, she is rewarded with a second chance to accept him. Elizabeth rejects the cynical *realpolitik* of the marriage market as expounded and practised by Charlotte Lucas; she also survives unscathed the temptations of the erotically attractive but immoral male, represented by Wickham. Wickham demonstrates his dangerous power on Elizabeth's younger sister, Lydia, and Darcy's moral rescue operation in this crisis precipitates his union with the grateful and admiring Elizabeth – a good example of the displacement of the Richardsonian seduction plot on to secondary characters. Something similar happens at the end of *Mansfield Park*, where the adultery of Henry Crawford with Maria Bertram and Mary Crawford's failure to condemn it 'justify' Fanny's earlier refusal of Crawford and precipitate her union with Edmund. The peripeteia (the surprising but satisfying reversal of expectation) in Jane Austen's plots very frequently takes the form of sexual misbehaviour, or something like it (such as Lucy Steele's marriage to Robert Ferrars in *Sense and Sensibility*).

The classic love story consists of a delay not only of the heroine's desire but also of the reader's desire – to know the answer to the basic question raised by the narrative: will the heroine get the man she wants? There are three principal sources of interest in narrative: suspense, mystery and irony. Suspense raises the question: what will happen? Mystery raises the question: why did it happen? When the reader knows the answer to the questions but the characters do not, irony is generated. Thus, all rereadings of novels tend to create an effect of irony, but this is especially true of Jane Austen's novels, which are permeated with irony, rhetorical as well as dramatic, and which can sustain an infinite number of readings. On first reading they tend, like most love stories, to engage the reader's interest through suspense rather than mystery. *Emma* is an exception, since it is full of enigmas (Why is Mr Elton so keen to attend the Westons' dinner party when Harriet is ill? Who sent the piano to Jane Fairfax? What are Frank Churchill's real feelings about Emma?) This follows from the fact that Emma does not fall in love until the book is almost over; therefore, the question: will she get the man she wants? cannot provide the main source of narrative interest. In *Pride and Prejudice*, too, though to a lesser extent, the heroine's knowledge of her own heart is delayed, and enigmas, mainly to do with Wickham and Darcy, supply narrative interest, together with the suspense plot concerning Bingley's intention toward Elizabeth's sister Jane. In the other novels Jane Austen makes relatively little use of mystery as a means of engaging the reader's interest, and in *Northanger Abbey* she mocked Mrs Radcliffe's rather mechanical reliance on this device in *The Mysteries of Udolpho* (1794).

In *Northanger Abbey*, Jane Austen played a delightful (and risky) double game with both the conventions of the sentimental novel and the conventions of traditional romance that were beginning to reinvade it through the contemporary cult of the Gothic – a process in which Mrs Radcliffe played a crucial role. At first sight, Jane Austen seems to be simply justifying the former at the expense of the latter. The famous conclusion to chapter 5, in which the narrator defends the novel as a form 'in which the greater powers of the mind are displayed, in which the most thorough knowledge of human nature, the happiest delineation of its varieties, the liveliest effusions of wit and humour are conveyed to the world in the best chosen language' (*NA*, p. 38),[1] explicitly cites titles by Fanny Burney and Maria Edgeworth. Catherine's naive addiction to the Gothic novel retards the happy consummation of her love for Henry Tilney – first, by leading her into uncritical friendship with Isabella Thorpe and her brother John, whose intrigues constantly threaten her happiness, and second, by tempting Catherine into a ludicrous suspicion, during her stay at Northanger Abbey, of General Tilney's having murdered his wife, thus herself temporarily forfeiting Henry's good opinion.

But as several commentators have observed, Catherine's opinion of the general is not totally unwarranted, since he shows himself to be a thoroughly nasty man. Furthermore, the conventions of the more realistic sentimental novel are themselves subjected to ironic undermining – none more devastating than the passage in which the narrator tells us that Henry Tilney's affection for Catherine 'originated in nothing better than gratitude, or, in other words, that a persuasion of her partiality for him had been the only cause of giving her a serious thought' (*NA*, p. 243); and none more witty than the narrator's admission that the anxiety of Henry and Catherine about the general's opposition to their marriage 'can hardly extend, I fear, to the bosom of my readers, who will see in the tell-tale compression of the pages before them, that we are all hastening together to perfect felicity' (*NA*, p. 250). It seems that there is no great 'virtue' in this heroine, and the narration of her 'reward' is almost contemptuously offhand, making the reader feel guilty at the pleasure he takes in it and sending him back, perhaps, to reread that highly equivocal defence of the novel as a genre in chapter 5.

Of all Jane Austen's novels *Northanger Abbey* is the only one that lends itself to a modern deconstructive reading, for it does seem to deny the reader any sure ground for interpretation and discrimination and to make explicit the impossibility of getting the world into a book. The other novels take the paradigm of the didactic love story more seriously, invest it with deeper significance, and centre it on heroines of more worth than Catherine Morland – but without sacrificing comedy and humour.

Comedy is not easily combined with the sentimental novel. *Pamela* is only unintentionally funny, a weakness Henry Fielding riotously exploited in *Shamela* (1741) and *Joseph Andrews* (1742). His own most sentimental novel, *Amelia* (1751), is his least amusing. In Richardson's *Clarissa* (1747–8) and in Rousseau's *La Nouvelle Héloïse* (1761), the sentimental pursuit of personal authenticity leads to tragedy, or at least pathos, to gestures of renunciation and loss, in which neither Jane Austen nor her heroines are interested. Emma's happiness – her eventual marriage to Knightley – entails disappointment for Harriet Smith, whose misplaced hopes of marrying him were unintentionally encouraged by Emma herself. Emma is sorry for Harriet, but not extravagantly so:

> For as to any of that heroism of sentiment which might have prompted her to entreat [Knightley] to transfer his affection from herself to Harriet, as infinitely the most worthy of the two – or even the more simple sublimity of resolving to refuse him at once and for ever, without vouchsafing any motive, because he could not marry them both, Emma had it not.

> (p. 431)

Both Fanny Burney and Maria Edgeworth leavened the sentimental novel with comedy, and Jane Austen undoubtedly learned from them; but their comedy is, compared with hers, more in the nature of 'comic relief' from the main story and often takes a rather robust, farcical form reminiscent of the comic fiction of Fielding, Sterne and Smollett, which itself derived ultimately from Rabelais, Cervantes and the picaresque tradition. Jane Austen's comedy seems more theatrical in its origins, reminding us faintly of Congreve, Molière and even Shakespeare.

One of the most venerable distinctions in general poetics is that drawn by Plato in Book III of *The Republic*, between diegesis (description of actions by an authorial narrator) and mimesis (representation of action through the imitated speech of characters). Drama is pure mimesis, in this sense, but the epic, and the novel which formally derives from it, combine diegesis and mimesis. Among the classic novelists, Jane Austen tends toward a dominantly mimetic method. Her stories are unfolded in a series of scenes, with a minimum of authorial description, and her skill in revealing character through speech is justly celebrated. Many passages from the earlier novels (e.g. the discussion between Mr and Mrs John Dashwood in chapter 3 of *Sense and*

Sensibility, and the dialogues between Mr and Mrs Bennet in *Pride and Prejudice*) could be performed as written (and have been, on radio, television and film). Action, in Jane Austen's novels, is social interaction of people in pairs, in groups, in social situations such as parties, dinners, balls, courtesy calls, walks and excursions – situations that lend themselves naturally to 'scenic' presentation and emphasize 'manners'. This is one reason why the comedy in Jane Austen does not seem tacked on to the love story but permeates it. This is true even of *Mansfield Park*, the most earnest of the novels and often disliked on that account. The comings and goings in the 'wilderness' at Sotherton (rather reminiscent of Shakespeare's Forest of Arden), for instance, and the whole saga of the theatricals, are exquisitely comic in a highly dramatic way, culminating in the wonderfully funny moment when the astonished Sir Thomas Bertram, unexpectedly returned home from the West Indies, interrupts Mr Yates rehearsing his part in *Lovers' Vows*:

> He stept to the door . . . and opening it, found himself on the stage of a theatre, and opposed to a ranting young man, who appeared likely to knock him down backwards. At the very moment of Yates perceiving Sir Thomas, and giving perhaps the very best start he had ever given in the whole course of his rehearsals, Tom Bertram entered at the other end of the room; and never had he found greater difficulty in keeping his countenance. His father's looks of solemnity and amazement on this his first appearance on any stage, and the gradual metamorphosis of the impassioned Baron Wildenhaim into the well-bred and easy Mr. Yates, making his bow and apology to Sir Thomas Bertram, was such an exhibition, such a piece of true acting as he would not have lost on any account. It would be the last – in all probability the last scene on that stage; but he was sure there could not be a finer.
>
> (pp. 182–3)

Here Jane Austen very characteristically turns the conventions of a falsifying kind of art inside out in order to reinforce the truthfulness of her own representation of experience. The encounter between Mr Yates and Sir Thomas takes place on the interface between life and art and is equally disconcerting to both parties on that account. Sir Thomas walks unintentionally on to a stage for the first time in his life and becomes willy-nilly an actor in a scene, just as Yates is startled by the reality of the encounter out of the artificial rant and exaggerated gesture of melodrama into a genuine 'start' from which he recovers by a piece of 'true' social acting. The touch of genius in the passage is, however, the introduction of Tom Bertram as a kind of audience for this piece of real-life theatre. It is through his eyes that we see and relish the ironies of the spectacle – and to recognize that fact is to recognize that, scenic as it is, Jane Austen's fiction is an achievement of narrative, not dramatic art. This kind of focalizing of the action through an individual viewpoint is peculiar to written narrative and is one of the constituents of fictional 'realism'.

The realism of Jane Austen's novels, the illusion of life that they create, has always been one of the chief attractions of her work to many generations of readers, from Sir Walter Scott's tribute, in his journal of 1826, to 'the exquisite touch, which renders ordinary commonplace things and characters interesting, from the truth of the description and the sentiment', to Arnold Kettle's declaration, in 1951, that '*Emma* is as convincing as our own lives, and has the same sort of concreteness'.[2] More recently, realism as a literary effect has fallen into disfavour. Post-structuralist criticism, especially that which derives from the work of Roland Barthes, has identified the 'classic realist text' as an instrument of ideology, a genre founded on bad faith, on the pretence that bourgeois culture is 'natural', using the dominance of the authorial voice over all the other discourses in the text to limit meaning in the interests of control, repression and privilege. It cannot be denied that Jane Austen took for granted the existence of class-society (though she did not see it as fixed or static), that she subscribed to the Christian-humanist notion of the autonomy and responsibility of the individual self, and that her novels unequivocally endorse certain values and reject others. If these are grounds for condemnation, then she stands condemned – though it seems a perverse and anachronistic judgement. Jane Austen's admirers have, however, often seemed handicapped in defending and celebrating her art by the poverty of their critical tools for analysing it. Without a metalanguage (a language for talking about an object language – in this case the language of literary realism), criticism is apt to find itself reduced to mere paraphrase, retelling Jane Austen's stories in language that is of the same kind as hers but inferior in eloquence, precision, and wit. Part of the problem is that realism is a literary effect that works by disguising its own conventionality. Some of the concepts and methods of structuralist and formalist criticism may help us to see through that disguise and understand how Jane Austen constructs a fictional world 'as convincing as our own lives'.

For example, Roland Barthes's analysis of the classic realist text in *S/Z* as a 'braiding' of multiple codes of signification – some having to do with the raising and resolution of narrative questions, some contributing to the creation of character, others imparting through devices of connotation the underlying themes and values of the story – all bound together in a kind of aesthetic 'solidarity', so that any segment of the text can be shown to be communicating several messages simultaneously: this would seem to be highly relevant to Jane Austen's fiction, in which every detail, every nuance of gesture and conversation, is charged with significance. One must make the reservation, however, that the codes of connotation in Jane Austen operate under much stricter constraints and offer the critic much less opportunity for exegetical display than Balzac (the subject of *S/Z*). Another way of putting this is to say that Jane Austen's novels exhibit in a very pure form the dominance of metonymy over metaphor that Roman Jakobson argued is characteristic of realism as a literary mode.[3] Metonymy is a trope that works by manipulating relationships of contiguity (as opposed to metaphor, which manipulates relationships of similarity). 'Metonymic' discourse thus emphasizes sequence and causality, and Jane Austen's novels illustrate this bias very well. Her novels have a seamless quality, one episode leading logically and naturally to the next. She is particularly artful in the way she introduces, or reintroduces, one character to fill the space left in the story by another. Thus, in *Emma*, when the enigma of Mr Elton's equivocal behaviour toward Emma and Harriet is solved to their mutual embarrassment and mortification and he departs from Highbury in a huff, the advent of Jane Fairfax and Frank Churchill, heralded many pages previously, provides a new focus of attention; and when Churchill, in turn, leaves the scene of Highbury, back comes Mr Elton with Mrs Elton (whom he has very plausibly married on the rebound from Emma). The reader of Jane Austen never feels, as he so often does with classic fiction, that the action has been patently contrived, new characters invented, new settings provided, to satisfy the exigencies of the plot and theme or simply to preserve the momentum of the text. Motivation of character conforms scrupulously to a code of psychological causality. In reading sentimental fiction by Jane Austen's contemporaries, one's credulity is frequently strained by the ability of hero and heroine to misunderstand each other (Fanny Burney's *Camilla* is a particularly flagrant example of a novel kept going, for some nine hundred pages, virtually by this means alone); but the mistakes and misjudgements of Jane Austen's characters satisfy the modern reader's most stringent standards of plausibility.

Metaphor and metaphorical symbolism are used very sparingly by Jane Austen, and under strict constraints. Mark Schorer showed how, in *Emma*, buried or 'dead' metaphors drawn from the language of commerce and property imply a scale of values that contrasts ironically, and almost subliminally, with the emotional and moral issues to which they are applied,[4] and I have written elsewhere about the extraordinarily subtle and delicate way in which the pathetic fallacy is used in the same novel to mark the transition of the heroine from despair to joy.[5] Even in *Persuasion*, by general consent the most 'poetic' or 'romantic' of the novels, the seasonal symbolism that attaches to the heroine's progress from an autumnal mood of resignation to a joyful 'second spring of youth and beauty' (*P*, p. 124) arises metonymically out of the actual seasonal span of the main action; and the metaphor of 'bloom' that articulates this theme most insistently (Anne is said to have lost her bloom at the beginning of the novel but to have recovered it by the end) is so conventional as scarcely to be perceived as a figurative expression.

One of the most fruitful concepts in modern narrative theory has been the Russian formalist distinction between *fabula* (the story as it would have been enacted in real time and space) and *sjuzet* (the story as it is represented in the text). In the case of fiction (as distinct from historiography), the *fabula* is not a prior reality but an extrapolation from the *sjuzet*, to be used as a tool of comparison. By observing how the narrative text selects, manipulates and 'deforms' the raw material of the *fabula*, we can uncover the formal choices that realistic illusion tends to disguise and relate those choices to the thematic and affective properties of the text. These choices crucially concern the handling of time, and what in Anglo-American criticism is loosely called 'point of view' (loosely, because it concerns not merely the perspective from which the action is seen but also the voice in which it is narrated).

Gérard Genette has identified three categories of time in which there may be more or less disparity between *fabula* and *sjuzet*: order, duration and frequency.[6] Jane Austen's narratives rarely deviate from chronological order. If there is a retrospective account of some event antecedent to the main action or a delayed explanation of some event in the main action, either it is incorporated into the time span of the main action in the form of a letter (e.g. Darcy's letter to Elizabeth explaining his involvement with Wickham; *PP*, pp. 196–203) or in dialogue (e.g. Willoughby's apologetic confession to Elinor; *SS*, pp. 319–20), or it is briefly summarized in a non-scenic way by the authorial narrator (e.g. the account of Anne Elliot's former relationship with Wentworth at the beginning of chapter 4 of *Persuasion*). In other words, there is a minimal disturbance of chronological order in Jane Austen's novels. We don't encounter in them the effect of flashback, in which the temporal progress of the main action is suspended and for a while effaced by the scenic presentation of an earlier event; nor do we encounter anything like a 'flashforward' – a proleptic glimpse of what is to come. The former effect is characteristic of fiction in which reality is seen as highly subjective – *Tristram Shandy*, for example, or the modern stream-of-consciousness novel; the latter effect is one in which the author as omniscient maker and manipulator of the fiction is apt to show his hand. By eschewing both these effects, Jane Austen strengthens the correspondence between her fictional world and the public, 'common-sense' notion of time as a plane on which we all move, from a known past toward an unknown future, according to a logic of causality that becomes intelligible only in retrospect.

By 'duration' Genette means the relationship between the time putatively occupied by the action of the *fabula* and the 'reading time' it is accorded in the text. The main action of Jane Austen's novels never occupies more than a year, and usually rather less. *Emma*, for instance, begins with Mrs Weston's marriage in the autumn and ends with the heroine's marriage the following autumn. *Persuasion* begins in autumn and ends the following spring. *Mansfield Park* stands out from the other novels in having a longish prelude describing Fanny's background and how she was adopted as a young child by the Bertram family, but the main action properly begins with the arrival of the Crawfords at *Mansfield Park* 'in the month of July, and Fanny had just reached her eighteenth year' (*MP*, p. 40). It ends the following summer. Why is there this consistency in the time span of Jane Austen's novels? Perhaps six months is about the shortest time in which to portray plausibly the development of a meaningful relationship between hero and heroine, particularly if it entails a revolution in feeling, as in Elizabeth Bennet's attitude to Darcy, Edmund Bertram's to Mary Crawford and Fanny, Wentworth's to Anne Elliot; and anything longer than twelve months would draw attention to ellipses in the temporal continuity of the narrative and slacken its grip on the reader.

The tempo of a fictional narrative can seem faster than reality (e.g. the thriller) or slower (the stream-of-consciousness novel) or to move at about the same pace. Jane Austen's novels seem to have the tempo of life itself, yet their stories occupy several months, and the reading of them takes only a few hours. The illusion is achieved by the highly selective and dominantly scenic presentation of experience. Jane Austen notoriously – it is one of the chief causes of critical controversy about her – left out a great deal from her novels: physical love, the work men do, historical events, 'local colour'. Her novels are concerned with the personal and social relations of young middle-class women confined to a very limited field of activity. The plot, which is concerned ultimately with the choice of husband, is furthered in a series of social encounters or 'scenes' that, because of the amount of direct speech in them, create the effect of more or less neutral duration, neither noticeably slower or faster than the tempo of 'reality'; and because of the habitual, repetitive quality of these scenes, we are scarcely aware of the intervals between them.

Consider, for example, the events in the second volume of *Emma* (chapters 19–36 in most modern editions): Emma and Harriet visit the Bateses and hear of Jane Fairfax's impending arrival; they visit again and meet Jane; Knightley calls at Hartfield, and so does Miss Bates, with news of Mr Elton's marriage; Harriet visits the Martins; Frank Churchill arrives and visits Hartfield and walks in the village with Emma; all the principal characters meet at the Coles's dinner party; Emma, Harriet, Mrs Weston and Frank Churchill call on the Bateses; discussions take place at Randalls and the Crown Inn about the proposed ball; Frank Churchill, summoned by his aunt, calls at Hartfield to say goodbye; Emma meets Mrs Elton and gives a dinner party in her honour. Two or three months have passed, yet we have no sense of the acceleration of the normal tempo of life.

By 'frequency', Genette refers to the ratio between the number of times an event occurs in the *fabula* and the number of times it is narrated in the *sjuzet*. As we might expect, Jane Austen generally follows the historical, 'common-sense' norm of one-to-one. She does, however, use summary (narrating once what happened several times) in linking passages and to express with sometimes disconcerting candour the tedium and repetitiveness of the social round to which her heroines are confined – for example, 'that kind of intimacy must be submitted to, which consists of sitting an hour or two together in the same room almost every day' (*SS*, p. 124). Jane Austen seldom repeats the narrative presentation of a single event, unless we count Emma's reflections on the Elton-Harriet débâcle (*E*, pp. 134–9) or Edmund's and Fanny's inquests on the behaviour of Mary Crawford (*MP*, pp. 63–4). She never presents successive accounts of the same event as experienced by two or more characters, in the manner of Richardson. This brings us to the topic of 'point of view'.

The great advantage of Richardson's epistolary technique – and the reason it enjoyed such a vogue – was that it short-circuited the simple alternation of diegesis and mimesis, author's voice and characters' voices, in traditional narrative by making the characters tell their own story virtually as it happened. The gain in immediacy and realistic illusion was enormous, but the technique had certain disadvantages, which, we may speculate, caused Jane Austen to abandon it after some early experiments. The machinery of correspondence was clumsy, uneconomical, and likely to strain credulity, while the elimination of the authorial voice from the text deprived it of an important channel of meaning. The nineteenth-century novel developed a new and more flexible combination of author's voice and characters' voices than the simple alternation of the two one finds in traditional epic narration, from Homer to Fielding and Scott – a discourse that fused, or interwove, them, especially through the stylistic device known as 'free indirect speech'. This technique, which Jane Austen was the first English novelist to use extensively, consists of reporting the thoughts of a character in language that approximates more or less closely to their own idiolect and deleting the introductory tags, such as 'he thought', 'she wondered', 'he said to himself' and the like, that grammar would normally require in the well-formed sentence. For instance, after Mr Elton's unwelcome declaration to Emma, the next chapter begins: 'The hair was curled, and the maid sent away, and Emma sat down to think and be miserable. – It was a wretched business, indeed! – Such an overthrow of every thing she had been wishing for! – Such a development of every thing most unwelcome! – Such a blow for Harriet! That was the worst of all' (*E*, p. 134). Free indirect speech, which enters this passage at the second sentence, allows the novelist to give the reader intimate access to a character's thoughts without totally surrendering control of the discourse to that character (as in the epistolary novel). The passage continues in a more summary and syntactically complex style, in which the narrator's judicial authority is perceptible, though Emma's consciousness remains focal:

> Every part of it brought pain and humiliation, of some sort or other; but, compared with the evil to Harriet, all was light; and she would gladly have submitted to feel yet more mistaken – more in error – more disgraced by mis-judgement, than she actually was, could the effects of her blunders have been confined to herself.

> (*E*, p. 134)

Free indirect speech, combined with presentation of the action from the spatio-temporal perspective of an individual character (the usual meaning of 'point of view' in literary criticism) allows the novelist to vary, from sentence to sentence, the distance between the narrator's discourse and the character's discourse, between the character's values and the 'implied author's' values, and so to control and direct the reader's affective and interpretive responses to the unfolding story. Thus, for instance, we identify, and identify with, Elinor rather than Marianne as the heroine of *Sense and Sensibility* because we see much more of the action from Elinor's perspective, because we have much more access to her private thoughts, and because there is much greater consonance between the narrator's language and the language of Elinor's consciousness. Marianne's unhappiness at Willoughby's desertion is consistently ironized, implicitly judged as self-indulgent, by an authorial rhetoric of oxymoron: 'this nourishment of grief was every day applied. She spent whole hours at the pianoforté alternately singing and crying' (p. 83); 'in such moments of precious, of invaluable misery, she rejoiced in tears of agony to be at Cleveland' (p. 303). Compare Elinor, confronted with apparent proof of Lucy Steele's engagement to Edward Ferrars: 'for a few moments, she was almost overcome – her heart sunk within her, and she could hardly stand; but exertion was indispensably necessary, and she struggled so resolutely against the oppression of her feelings, that her success was speedy, and for the time complete' (p. 134).

There is considerable variation between the novels in the amount of switching from one character's perspective to another's and in the degree to which the narrator explicitly invokes her authority and omniscience. In *Pride and Prejudice*, for instance, such effects are frequent. Although Elizabeth is the dominant centre of interest, and consciousness, the narrative frequently moves away from her perspective. Here is a characteristic shift:

> Occupied in observing Mr. Bingley's attentions to her sister, Elizabeth was far from suspecting that she was herself becoming an object of some interest in the eyes of his friend. Mr. Darcy had at first scarcely allowed her to be pretty . . . But no sooner had he made it clear to himself and his friends that she had hardly a good feature in her face, than he began to find it was rendered uncommonly intelligent by the beautiful expression of her dark eyes.

> (*PP*, p. 23)

It is important to the effect of the novel that the reader should know this and Elizabeth should not. A little later in the same scene, Elizabeth is 'eagerly succeeded' at the piano by her sister Mary.

> Mary had neither genius nor taste; and though vanity had given her application, it had given her likewise a pedantic air and conceited manner, which

would have injured a higher degree of excellence than she had reached. Elizabeth, easy and unaffected, had been listened to with much more pleasure, though not playing half so well.

(*PP*, p. 25)

This brutally frank comparison of the sisters comes to us straight from the authorial narrator, and Elizabeth is not compromised, here or elsewhere, by any suspicion of vanity or disloyalty to her mostly tiresome family. Throughout the novel the reader is put in a privileged position of knowing more than any of the characters know individually.

Emma follows an antithetical method. It is quite true to say, as F.R. Leavis did, that 'everything is presented through Emma's dramatised consciousness'.[7] There are two important scenes in which Emma is not present and therefore, axiomatically, cannot provide the point of view. The first of these is chapter 5 of volume 1, a dialogue between Mr Knightley and Mrs Weston about Emma that remains wholly 'objective' until the last paragraph, which gives us a hint of Mrs Weston's private hopes of a match between Emma and Frank Churchill. In the fifth chapter of volume 3, there is a shift of point of view to Knightley, when he begins to suspect Frank Churchill of 'some double dealing in his pursuit of Emma' (p. 343) and 'of some inclination to trifle with Jane Fairfax'. (In the following chapter Mrs Elton plans her strawberry-picking expedition when Emma is absent, but this scene is less important hermeneutically.) There are also some very clear authorial comments about Emma's character at the outset of the novel that should put the reader on his guard against identifying too readily with her attitudes and opinions: for example, 'The real evils indeed of Emma's situation were the power of having rather too much her own way, and a disposition to think a little too well of herself' (p. 5). But with these reservations it is true that the action of the novel is narrated wholly from Emma's perspective, so that the reader is obliged, on first reading at least, to share her limited knowledge and perhaps her mistakes and surprises. There is, to my knowledge, no precedent for such a novel before *Emma* – that is, a novel in which the authorial narrator mediates virtually all the action through the consciousness of an unreliable focalizing character. The effect is not only a wonderful multiplication of ironies and reversals but also an intensification of what Henry James called the sense of felt life – a more intimate relationship between fictional discourse and the processes of human consciousness. And not until Henry James himself, perhaps, was there a novelist in the English language who equalled the skill and subtlety with which Jane Austen carried out this difficult technical feat. To make that comparison inevitably recalls the astonishing perversity of James's own observation that 'Jane Austen was instinctive and charming ... For signal examples of what composition, distribution, arrangement can do, of how they intensify the life of a work of art, we have to go elsewhere.'[8] He never said an untruer word.

Notes on Composition, distribution, arrangement

1 All page references to Jane Austen's novels are to the third editions of the texts edited by R.W. Chapman, Oxford, 1932–4.

2 Arnold Kettle, *An Introduction to the English Novel*, 1962, p. 100.

3 Roman Jakobson, 'Two aspects of language and two types of linguistic disturbances', in Roman Jakobson and Morris Halle, *Fundamentals of Language*, The Hague, 1956. See also my *The Modes of Modern Writing*, London, 1977.

4 Mark Schorer, 'The humiliation of Emma Woodhouse', reprinted in *Emma: A Casebook*, ed. D. Lodge, 1968.

5 Introduction to *Emma*, Oxford, 1971, pp. xiv–xvi.

6 Gérard Genette, *Narrative Discourse*, trans. J.E. Lewin, Oxford, 1980.

7 F.R. Leavis, *The Great Tradition*, 1948, p. 19n.

8 Henry James, *The House of Fiction*, ed. Leon Edel, 1957, p. 207.

Further reading

Becker, Howard S. (1998) *Tricks of The Trade: How To Think About Your Research While You're Doing It*. Chicago Guides to Writing, Editing and Publishing. Chicago and London: University of Chicago Press.

Butrym, Alexander J. (ed.) (1989) *Essays on the Essay: Redefining the Genre*. Athens: University of Georgia Press.

Cockcroft, R. and Cockcroft, Susan M. (1992) *Persuading People: An Introduction to Rhetoric*. London: Macmillan.

Crème, P. and Lea, Mary R. (1997) *Writing at University: A Guide for Students*. Buckingham: Open University Press.

Crosswhite, J. (1996) *The Rhetoric of Reason: Writing and the Attractions of Argument*. Madison: University of Wisconsin Press.

Fabb, N. and Durant, A. (1993) *How to Write Essays, Dissertations and Theses in Literary Studies*. Harlow: Longman.

Grabe, William and Kaplan, Robert (1996) *Theory and Practice of Writing*. Harlow: Longman.

Gross, John (ed.) (1991) *The Oxford Book of Essays*. Oxford: Oxford University Press.

The Hutchinson Book of Essays. London: Hutchinson, 1990.

Johnson, J. (1987) *The Bedford Guide to the Research Process*. Bedford: St Martins.

Leki, Ilona (1998) *Academic Writing: Exploring Processes And Strategies*, 2nd edn. Cambridge: Cambridge University Press.

McCuen, Jo Ray and Winkler, A.C. (1991) *Reading, Writing, and the Humanities*. San Diego and London: Harcourt Brace Jovanovich.

Raimes, A. (1992) *Exploring through Writing: A Process Approach to ESL Composition*. New York: St Martins Press.

Rasool, Joan, Banks, Caroline and McCarthy, Mary-Jane (1996) *Critical Thinking: Reading and Writing in a Diverse World*. Belmont and London: Wadsworth.

Summers, Vivian (1991) *Clear English*. London: Penguin.

Ward, Russ (1997) *Logical Argument in the Research Paper*. Fort Worth and London: Harcourt Brace College Publishers.

Index

Learning Resources
Centre